The Learning Power of Laughter

by Jackie Silberg

Dedication

This book is dedicated to the joy of laughter.

Acknowledgments

I would like to thank my editor, Kathy Charner, for her wonderful wit and great editing. We have written so many books together, and she has always made the journey very special.

For Leah and Larry Rood, I thank you for believing in my ideas and for the wonderful support that you give me.

Special thanks go to Heidi Estrin who is a children's librarian in Florida and to Zanni Van Antwerp who is a classroom teacher in Nevada. They contributed some excellent activities to this book.

> "When your belly starts to shake and your funny bone starts to ache, you can rattle and roll, but you sure can't fake, 'cause once you start laughing, your whole body's awake!"
> ~Richard Simmons

Other books by the author:

125 Brain Games for Babies: Simple Games to Promote Early Brain Development

125 Brain Games for Toddlers and Twos: Simple Games to Promote Early Brain Development

300 Three Minute Games: Quick and Easy Activities for 2-5 Year Olds

500 Five Minute Games: Quick and Easy Activities for 3-6 Year Olds

All About Me

Brain Games for Babies, Toddlers, and Twos: 140 Fun Ways to Boost Development

The Complete Book of Activities, Games, Stories, Props, Recipes, and Dances for Young Children

The Complete Book of Rhymes, Songs, Poems, Fingerplays, and Chants: Over 700 Selections

Games to Play With Babies, Third Edition

Games to Play With Toddlers, Revised

Games to Play With Two-Year-Olds, Revised

Go Anywhere Games for Babies

Hello Rhythm: Rhythm Activities, Songs, and Games to Develop Skills

Hello Sound: Creative Music Activities for Parents and Teachers of Young Children

Higglety, Pigglety, Pop!: 233 Playful Rhymes and Chants

The I Can't Sing Book: For Grownups Who Can't Carry a Tune in a Paper Bag… But Want to Do Music With Young Children

I Live in Kansas

I Love Children Songbook

Let's Be Friends

Lollipops and Spaghetti Activity Book: Developmental Activities

My Toes Are Starting to Wiggle and Other Easy Songs for Circle Time

Peanut Butter, Tarzan, and Roosters Activity Book

Sing Yeladim

Sniggles, Squirrels, and Chickenpox: 40 Original Songs With Activities for Early Childhood

Songs to Sing With Babies

The Learning Power of laughter

Over 300 Playful Games, Activities, and Ideas That Promote Learning With Young Children

gryphon house, inc.
Beltsville, MD 20704

Jackie Silberg

Library of Congress Cataloging-in-Publication

Silberg, Jackie, 1934-
  The learning power of laughter / by Jackie Silberg.
     p. cm.
  Includes bibliographical references and index.
  ISBN 0-87659-268-X
1. Early childhood education--Activity programs. 2. Educational games.
3. Laughter. I. Title.
LB1139.A37S55 2004
372.13--dc22

                                            2004002434

Bulk purchase

Gryphon House books are available for special premiums and sales promotions as well as for fund-raising use. Special editions or book excerpts also can be created to specification. For details, contact the Director of Marketing at Gryphon House.

Disclaimer

Gryphon House, Inc. and the author cannot be held responsible for damage, mishap, or injury incurred during the use of or because of activities in this book. Appropriate and reasonable caution and adult supervision of children involved in activities and corresponding to the age and capability of each child involved, is recommended at all times. Do not leave children unattended at any time. Observe safety and caution at all times.

Table of Contents

Chapter 4—Imagination Games and Activities   61

Chapter 5—Active Games and Activities   73

Chapter 6—Group Games and Activities 91

The Serious Side of Silly

Several years ago, I interviewed for a teaching position with the Los Angeles City Schools. I took many written tests, and I spoke to several department heads in the school district. They asked me many questions about my philosophy on education, how I would handle certain stressful situations, and what I thought was the most important quality of a good teacher. My answer to the last question was "a sense of humor." Later, I learned that the interviewers loved my answer to that question.

I believe that laughter has the power to heal and the power to teach. I believe that humor is a vital part of teachers' and children's educational experience. And, many years ago, after reading Norman Cousins' book, *Anatomy of an Illness as Perceived by the Patient*, I knew that I had to write this book.

Norman Cousins was the Editor of the *Saturday Review of Literature*. He is often described as the man who laughed his way to health, a simplified explanation of the controversial healing method he used when he was diagnosed in the mid-1960's with ankylosing spondylitis. This degenerative disease causes the breakdown of collagen, the fibrous tissue that binds together the body's cells. Almost completely paralyzed, given only a few months to live, Cousins checked himself out of the hospital. He moved into a hotel room, began taking extremely high doses of vitamin C, and also exposed himself to equally high doses of humor, consisting of recordings, comedians who came to visit him, and movies.

Ultimately, Cousins regained use of his limbs. As his condition steadily improved over the following months, he resumed his busy life, eventually returning to work full-time at the *Saturday Review*. Cousins detailed his journey in "Anatomy of an Illness." I was so fascinated by his book, I continued looking for information about laughter and its importance. I learned even more what a difference it made in relationships with children as well as adults.

A sense of humor is learned. Just as children learn qualities of kindness or persistence by example, so, too, do children learn about humor. They model themselves after the adults in their lives. Parents with good senses of humor often have children who enjoy humor and are funny themselves. Having a good sense of humor and recognizing and taking opportunities for laughing out loud help develop good social skills and encourage the development of many other skills that children need, including pre-reading skills, creativity, and cognitive thinking.

Add More Laughter to Your Life

According to research, when a person laughs, carbon dioxide is driven out of the body and is replaced by oxygen-rich air. This produces anti-inflammatory agents, encouraging muscles to relax and exercising muscles all over the body, from the scalp to the legs, all while reducing levels of the stress hormone cortisol (*Choice Magazine*, March 2001).

The physiological study of laughter is called "gelotology," which tells us that laughter seems to be produced via a circuit that runs through many regions of the brain. According to Dr. Lee Berk and Dr. Stanley Tan of Loma Linda University in California, the three main areas are:

1. The cognitive thinking part of the brain helps you get the joke. This area is found in parts of the frontal lobe near the forehead.
2. The motor parts of the brain help move the muscles of the face to smile and laugh.
3. The emotional parts of the brain help produce the happy feelings that accompany a cheerful experience.

Increasingly, studies are demonstrating that laughter and humor boost immunity, diminish pain, and help people deal with the stress of life. Just a few fun experiences a week will elevate feel-good serotonin levels and help boost your immune system and improve your health.

Laughter, fun, and humor serve an important developmental function for young children as a way to express their growing powers of reasoning and creativity. The educational value of this bond is inestimable. Children will learn and retain more of what you teach them and you both will enjoy every minute of it. According to Dr. William Fry, professor emeritus at Stanford Medical School, "Laughter aids memory and increases alertness and concentration." (www.brain.com, "Laughter and the Brain").

Because so much learning power exists in a good laugh it is important to use this wonderful gift. Share your laughter and help make others laugh. Share your humorous perspective and give others permission to do the same. A good sense of humor is something everyone can work on. On the next page are a few suggestions to help add more laughter to your life:

> In India, there is a group of people called the Laugh Club who gather and laugh for a few minutes without stopping. Laughter is a powerful, wonderful thing. They are one of hundreds of Laugh Clubs throughout the world. Wouldn't it be wonderful to establish a time every week just to laugh!

BENEFITS OF LAUGHTER

★ **Laughter is good for you. When you laugh, chemicals called endorphins, which make you feel good, are released by the brain.**

★ **Laughter increases learning and retention. Laughing stimulates both sides of the brain. People get the message quicker and remember it longer.**

★ **Laughter stimulates the brain, the nervous system, the respiratory system, the hormonal system, and the muscular system. Studies show that it lowers blood pressure, decreases depression, increases muscle flexion, reduces allergy symptoms, strengthens the immune system, and reduces stress!**

★ **Laughter reduces pain. The endorphins released during laughter have been proven to help reduce pain and enhance treatments of many illnesses and diseases.**

★ **Laughter is a powerful force. Breath released during a hearty laugh has been clocked at speeds as fast as 170 miles per hour.**

★ **Laughter knows no cultural boundaries. You don't have to speak the same language to laugh together.**

★ **Laughter helps break the ice when you're in a group. It is the one form of communication to which everyone can relate.**

★ Recognize the value of humor.
★ Don't worry or analyze why people laugh—just participate.
★ Think funny—look for the humor in every situation. Learn to laugh at the incongruities in life.
★ Keep a notebook of funny things and write in it daily.
★ Adapt material. Use humor from any source. Personalize it and change it to suit your situation or the problem at hand.

Remember that laughter not only makes you feel better, but the use of humor can be a major tool for insight. George Burns said it best: "You can't help getting older, but you can help getting old. Chronologically, the clock is going to keep on ticking for all of us, but if we take a lick of humor, we can prevent a hardening of the attitudes. If we savor humor, humor can be a lifesaver" (*Home Extension Line Newsletter*, April 2001, Issue 3).

Young Children and Humor

When adults laugh, most often it is because they think something is funny. However, when children laugh, this may not be the case. Often, children are simply mimicking the laughter of adults or other children. This copycat laughter is another example of how children model their behavior on what they see and experience around them.

Young children do enjoy the incongruous. They like to string together rhyming words or nonsense syllables. Because language is supposed to be logical and orderly and sentences don't usually rhyme, it seems funny to children when they do. Children also enjoy the implausible or absurd—a cartoon of a fish wearing glasses or the sight of the family dog licking the dinner plates, for example. Almost anything that goes against what children consider normal and predictable can tickle their funny bones.

Because the idea of thumbing one's nose at the norm is so appealing to young children, bathroom humor is fairly common in this age group. Preschoolers know that certain words are unacceptable to adults, and they may use the words deliberately for shock value. In addition, a fine line exists between what is funny and what is frightening. That is why many little children are frightened by clowns, Santa, and costumed figures. When a clown appears wearing a red wig and face paint, children may be scared instead of amused. They may not be sure that this is really a person in disguise.

What Children Learn From All That Giggling

Young children have a special propensity toward silliness that, according to experts (*Christian Parenting Today*, 2002), has important developmental benefits for building social skills, cognitive thinking, and creativity. Laughter creates bonds between people. As children grow and their social world expands, they will use the link of silliness and laughter to solidify other friendships.

Stretching the imagination, thinking outside the box, and learning to look at a situation from different angles are other long-term benefits of developing a sense of humor. Child psychologist Niki Saros observes that children who are creative thinkers have a certain mental flexibility that allows them to escape from the pressure of a hyper-structured view of the world. That skill translates to creative problem solving down the road (*Christian Parenting Today*, Summer 2002).

According to kindergarten teacher Lauri Barrette, "There is purpose in silliness. The child is asserting his personality and trying to entertain those around him. He is learning through the responses what is socially appropriate and what is not."

FUNNY IDEAS TO USE WITH CHILDREN

When children see that adults can be playful, do "funny" things, and have a sense of humor, they will model this behavior. Laughing can keep things in perspective. How do you show your sense of humor? Here are some ideas from teachers and parents.

★ We made up silly rhyming jingles to go with our kids' names. My husband was exceptionally good at this. Our daughter's name is Andria. He called her: Andrioli Catoli Minnoli. Our son, Zach, was: Zachary Zoodley Doodley Oh. Zach is now 13 and one of many "Zachs". His nickname is still "Zoo"—a shortened version of his name jingle. Even at 13 and 15, these old name jingles still bring a smile to our kids.

★ Another thing that I did (and still do, although there aren't as many opportunities) was to record the cute, funny things the kids said and then I posted them on our kitchen cabinets. We called it the "quote board." I dated each quote and as the cabinets filled up with quotes, I took the quotes off the cabinet doors and stuck them in a journal. When each of my children turned 13, I created a memory book with one section that included all of their quotes from the quote board. We ALL get chuckles out of reading those.

★ Sometimes when my six-year-old is upset about something I will tell him that I used to be upset by the same thing when I was a child. I will then ask him if he would like to know what I did to help me through. He usually says yes, and I then tell him I did something silly —walked around the house clucking like a chicken or did a "hoochie-coochie" dance.

★ I wear a headband with two shamrocks on springs.

★ I often tell the children that I sleep at school (and there are times I truly feel that way!). I've considered greeting them at the door wearing a big housecoat, fuzzy slippers, curlers in my hair, and holding a coffee cup.

★ I've worn two different colored shoes, worn my sweater inside out for a whole day, and squirted yellow paint down the front of my white shirt. I told everyone I had mustard for breakfast. I think most of true humor comes from enjoying children—listening to the 100th knock-knock joke, letting them see me laugh at my inside-out sweater, and laughing when the paint spills all over me.

★ I love to dress up in costumes. The two most memorable were:

  ★ The Rainy Day Fairy: I dressed up in an evening gown, high heels, and a motorcycle helmet from the Housekeeping Center and carried a red vinyl bag filled with tissues. I walked from room to room and recited a little ditty in a silly opera lady voice:

  I'm the rainy day fairy and it's my job today
  To chase all the rainy day sadness away.
  I pranced out of the room tossing
  tissues like a flower girl.

  ★ This past year on May 1, I dressed up as April Showers. I wore a long bright yellow raincoat, dark sunglasses, a leftover Halloween wig from a party store, and flip-flops, and carried a bright umbrella. I said, "My name is April Showers, and I am her to bring you May flowers." I gave all the children "May" flowers and left. Then I took off my costume and went back to my room. The children couldn't wait to tell me all about "Mrs. Rain" and how she brought flowers.

★ We have backwards day when we wear our clothes backwards, walk backwards, and eat dessert first.

★ We have crazy hat and/or hair day.

★ We have "Horrible Hair Day" in honor of Mr. H from the Letter People. I gel up what little hair I have left and let it stick out in spikes.

Humor for Adults

We all deserve to laugh. The following poems and riddles will give you a chuckle. Enjoy and share them with your friends.

The Octopus
Tell me, Octopus, I begs
Is those things arms, or is they legs?
I marvel at thee, Octopus,
If I were thou, I'd call me Us.
—Ogden Nash

If You Should Meet a Crocodile
If you should meet a Crocodile,
Don't take a stick and poke him.
Ignore the welcome in his smile
Be careful not to stroke him.
For as he sleeps upon the Nile
He thinner gets and thinner.
And whene'er you meet a Crocodile
He's ready for his dinner.

Glowworm
Never talk down to a glowworm
Such as "What do you knowworm?"
How's it down belowworm?
Guess you're quite a slowworm
No, just say...helloworm!

I Often Pause and Wonder

I often pause and wonder
At fate's peculiar ways
For nearly all our famous men
Were born on holidays.

'Tis Dog's Delight

'Tis dog's delight to bark and bite
And little birds to sing
And if you sit on a red-hot brick
It's a sign of an early spring.

Don't Worry If Your Job Is Small

Don't worry if your job is small
And your rewards are few.
Remember that the mighty oak
Was once a nut like you!

She Wore Her Stockings Inside Out

She wore her stockings inside out
All through the summer heat.
She said it cooled her off to turn
The hose upon her feet.

As I Was Standing in the Street

As I was standing in the street
As quiet as could be,
A great big ugly man came up
And tied his horse to me.

Riddles for Adults

What kind of cat should you never play cards with?
...a cheetah

What do you see when the smog lifts in Los Angeles?
...UCLA

What would we have if all the cars in the nation were pink?
...a pink carnation

And Two Funny Tunes

(Tune: "God Save The King/Queen")
King George, he had a date,
He stayed out very late,
He was the King.
Queen Mary paced the floor,
King George came home at four,
She met him at the door—
God save the King.

No L
Sing to the tune of the "First Noel." Be sure to leave out the letter "L" as you sing the alphabet.

A B C D E F G
H I J K M N
O P Q R S T
U V W X Y Z
No L, no L, no L, no L,
No L, no L, no L, no L.

How to Use This Book

In this book you will find games, poems, songs, stories, fingerplays, riddles, tongue twisters, and jokes in many categories. All of them encourage laughter and fun, and at the same time, teach important developmental concepts. Find positive, creative ways for children to express humor. You can do this by showing appreciation for their jokes or funny stories, whether they mix up the details or forget the punch line. Also, read humorous stories to them, those that approach humor in upbeat, child-friendly ways, such as *If You Give a Pig a Pancake* by Laura Numeroff, *Pete's a Pizza* by William Steig, and *Stanley and Rhoda* by Rosemary Wells.

Each activity in this book contains a section called "Learning Power," which is a list of the important skills and concepts that children will learn as they participate in the activities. The following list of terms describes these skills and concepts in detail. Choose activities that focus on the skills you wish to emphasize.

Body Awareness: A good way to help children learn about their bodies is through fingerplays, movement games, poems, and other activities that relate to and identify various body parts. They become aware of all the amazing things their bodies can do.

Cognitive Thinking: This skill develops over time in children, as they learn to use factual knowledge to support their thoughts and beliefs. As they learn to ask and answer questions, they learn self-reliance and develop confidence in themselves.

Creativity/Imagination: A critical component of active young minds, a creative imagination stimulates children to learn more and in new ways. It encourages playfulness and supports problem-solving skills.

Dramatic play: This type of play supports creativity/imagination and developing language skills.

Emotions/Empathy: Children learn through laughter and play about the importance of respecting emotions and showing empathy for others.

Coordination: Games and activities that promote eye-hand coordination or gross or fine motor coordination give children an added benefit. Not only do they laugh and learn, but they also become aware of how to use their bodies effectively.

Letter recognition: Along with phonemic awareness, this skill is a vital part of the pre-reading process. As they laugh and play, children learn the 26 letters of the alphabet and begin to associate each letter with a different sound.

Listening: The importance of learning to listen cannot be overstated. In this book, children engage in many activities in which they must listen for certain cues and then respond, or listen to words with a careful ear in order to find the humor.

Observation: "Watch and learn." This expression describes the actions of curious children everywhere. As children watch experienced adults perform activities, such as writing, speaking, storytelling, and so on, they learn how to perform those same activities.

Phonemic Awareness: Learning the sounds of the 44 different phonemes is critical to becoming a successful reader. When children play with words, substituting different vowel or consonants in familiar words, they learn to associate letters with certain sounds. This skill helps children in later years when they need to decode words.

Rhyming: This is an important pre-reading skill, helping children learn specific "chunks" of words (bat, rat, cat) and supporting spelling and word identification skills.

Rhythm: Poetry is based on rhythm, and oral language takes on different rhythms depending on the speaker and the content of what is spoken. Children naturally tune in to rhythm and, in the process, they learn important language skills.

Sequencing: This skill is important for children to learn. When children are successful in answering the question, "What comes next?" they learn to recognize the order of events in stories and other informational materials, which builds overall reading comprehension skills.

Socialization: When children are encouraged to interact with their peers in playful, healthy contexts, they thrive in every way. Socially, they learn to get along with others and work in groups. As they learn these critical concepts, they also increase their vocabularies, become fluent communicators, and realize the joy that comes with having friendships and shared experiences with others.

Vocabulary: Increasing the vocabularies of young children before they can read enhances their later success as they become fluent readers.

Above all, laugh and learn along with young children!

Laughing With Language and Sounds

The games in this chapter help young children develop key skills that directly affect literacy. Pre-literacy activities are based on language acquisitions and are practiced through the day-to-day play of children. You can help children develop alliteration skills, phonemic awareness, rhyming, sequencing, and other important pre-reading skills just by being playful with words. Use the tongue twisters, silly sounds, jokes and riddles, knock-knock jokes, and the list of silly books and songs to add humor and laughter to each day.

Tongue Twisters

Tongue twisters develop language fluency, alliteration skills, letter recognition, and fun with words. Stringing together rhyming words or nonsense syllables is amusing and fun.

1. Andy ran to the Andies from the Indies in his undies.

2. Angela Abigail Applewhite ate anchovies and artichokes.

3. Ailing Auntie Annie Ames ate apple butter in abundance.

4. Bertha Bartholomew blew big, blue bubbles.

5. Betty Botter had some butter,
   "But," she said, "this butter's bitter.
   If I bake this bitter butter,
      It will make my batter bitter.
      But a bit of better butter—
         That would make my batter better."

      So she bought a bit of butter,
      Better than her bitter butter,
      And she baked it in her batter,
      And the batter was not bitter.
      So 'twas better Betty Botter
      Bought a bit of better butter.

6. The blue bluebird blinks.

7. Bobby brings bright bells.

8. Busy buzzing bumblebees.

9. Captain Kangaroo's carefully crunching crunchy candy corn.

10. Chilly chipper children cheerfully chant.

11. Do drop in at the Dewdrop Inn.

12. Double bubble gum doubles bubbles.

13. Dwayne Dwiddle drew a drawing of dreaded Dracula.

14. Eleven elves licked eleven little licorice lollipops.

15. A flea and a fly flew up in a flue.
    Said the flea, "Let us fly!"
    Said the fly, "Let us flee!"
    So they flew through a flaw in the flue.

16. Floyd Flingle flipped flat flapjacks.

17. Freshly fried fresh fish.

18. Gertie's great-grandma grew aghast at Gertie's grammar.

19. Gray geese graze in the green, green grass.

20. Greta Gruber grabbed a group of green grapes.

21. How much wood would a woodchuck chuck if a
        woodchuck could chuck wood?
    He would chuck, he would, as much as he could,
    And chuck as much wood as a woodchuck would,
    If a woodchuck could chuck wood.

22. Julie Jackson juggled the juicy,
    jiggly Jell-O.

23. Karl Kessler kept the ketchup in
    the kitchen.

24. Lila Ledbetter lugged a lot of little lemons.

25. Nat's knapsack strap snapped.

26. Norris Newton never needed new noodles.

27. Peter Piper picked a peck of pickled peppers.
    A peck of pickled peppers Peter Piper picked.
    If Peter Piper picked a peck of pickled peppers,
    Where's the peck of pickled peppers Peter Piper picked?

28. Pick up six pick-up sticks quickly.

29. Red lorry, yellow lorry, red lorry, yellow lorry.
    (a lorry is a truck in England)

30. Round and round the rugged rocks the ragged rascal ran.

31. Rubber baby buggy bumpers.

32. Sam shaved seven shy sheep. Seven shaved sheep shivered shyly.

33. Sam's sock shop stocks short spotted socks.

34. Seven Santas sang silly songs.

35. She sells seashells by the seashore.
    Where are the shells that she sells by the seashore?

36. Sheep shouldn't sleep in a shack.
    Sheep should sleep in a shed.

37. Shirley sewed Sly's shirt shut.

38. Six sick sheep. The sixth sick sheep is the sheik's sixth sheep.

39. Six thick thistle sticks. Six thick thistles stick.

40. A skunk sat on a stump.
    The skunk thunk the stump stunk,
    And the stump thunk the skunk stunk.

41. Swan, swan, over the sea,
    Swim, swan, swim.
    Swan, swan, back again,
    Well swum swan.

42. Tiny Timmy trims the tall tree with tinsel.

43. A tutor who tooted the flute
    Tried to tutor two tooters to toot.
    "Toot-toot!" said the tooters.
    "Tut-tut!" said the tutor.
    It's harder to tutor than toot.

44. Three grey geese on the green grass grazing.

45. Whether the weather be fine, or whether the weather be not,
Whether the weather be cold, or whether the weather be hot,
We'll weather the weather, whatever the weather, whether we like it
or not.

46. Zebras zig and zebras zag.

Short Tongue Twisters

Try to say the following three times fast.

Aluminum linoleum.
Black bugs' blood.
Greek grapes.
Lemon liniment.
Mixed biscuits.
Peggy Babcock.
Preshrunk shirts.
Short takes.
Soldier's shoulders.
Truly rural.
Yellow yo-yos.

ACTIVITIES TO DO WITH TONGUE TWISTERS

These fun activities will increase letter recognition.

Letter Tongue Twisters

1. Choose three or four tongue twisters.
2. Make a large letter to go with each rhyme: for example, B for Betty Botter, S for Swan, P for Peter Piper, etc.
3. The group sits in a circle on the floor.
4. Choose one of the tongue twisters and say it very slowly.
5. Encourage the group to repeat the rhyme one line at a time.
6. Reinforce alphabet skills by holding up the letter that goes with each rhyme. For example, hold up a large B for "Betty Botter."

Say-It-Again Game

1. Each player in the group takes a turn saying a tongue twister over and over again until he or she makes a mistake.
2. The player who repeats the twister the most times is the winner.
3. Use any tongue twister, but the ones that follow are especially hard to say more than once.

   ★ Which wristwatch is the Swiss wristwatch?
   ★ Red leather, yellow leather.
   ★ Double bubble gum doubles bubbles.
   ★ She sells seashells by the seashore.

Silly Sounds

Nourish a sense of humor and develop language skills, such as beginning and ending sounds, phonemes, imitation of sound, and discovering body sounds, by playing with silly sounds.

Airplane—drone an "oo" sound, then start to whistle at the same time. Try making your vocal sound go up and down as you are whistling.

Baby Burblers—push lips forward, say "boo," and flap lips with one finger.

Beat Box—cup mouth with hands and make up a typical pop rhythm out of mouth sounds.

Body Scratcher—scratch all over with one hand, while the other secretly scratches the underside of a table or chair.

Cheek Poppers—either put your finger in the side of your mouth and pop it out, or form an "O" with your lips and flick your cheek.

Ducks—roll tongue backwards onto the roof of your mouth and suck.

Ground Shaker—grit teeth, put tongue flat against the roof of your mouth and blow air out between your back teeth and your cheeks. Shake your head so that your cheeks flap, or pinch and flap them with your fingers. Precede all this with a slowly descending whistle.

Head Hopper—tap head with knuckles of one hand while secretly banging the underside of a table or chair with the other.

Raspberries—make a raspberry sound with your lips while you are making a sound with your voice.

Spine Shivers—stretch a blade of grass between your thumbs and blow through them.

Underarm Squelch—cup your hand over your armpit. Bring your arm down hard onto your hand to make a raspberry sound.

Jokes and Riddles

Encourage positive ways to express humor. You can do this by showing appreciation for jokes or funny stories, even when children get the details mixed up or forget the punch line. In addition to creating humorous moments, jokes and riddles also foster the development of speech and problem-solving skills.

1. Why is six afraid of seven?
   (Because seven "ate" nine)

2. What do you call two bananas?
   (A pair of slippers)

3. What do you call a sick alligator?
   (An illigator)

4. What do you call a baby whale?
   (A little squirt)

5. What do you call a bee that hums very quietly?
   (A mumblebee or a humblebee)

6. What do you call a freight train loaded with bubble gum?
   (A chew-chew train)

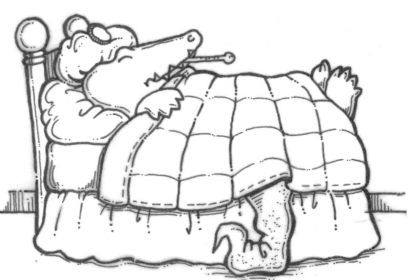

7. What do you call someone who carries an encyclopedia in his pocket?
   (Smarty-pants)

8. Why is it hard to talk with a goat around?
   (He keeps butting in.)

9. Why don't ducks tell jokes while they are flying?
   (They might quack up.)

10. There were 10 cats in a boat and one jumped out. How many were left?
    (None. They were copycats.)

11. What kind of bow can't be tied?
    (A rainbow)

12. Which pen won't write?
    (A pigpen)

13. What pool is no good for swimming?
    (A car pool)

14: Where do cows go on their space vacation?
    (The moooooon!)

15. What are cows' favorite party games?
    (MOO-sical chairs)

16. What do you get if you cross a flea with a rabbit?
    (Bugs Bunny)

17. Why do mother kangaroos hate rainy days?
    (Because the kids have to play inside)

18. What is a mouse's favorite game?
    (Hide and squeak)

19. How do you catch a squirrel?
    (Climb a tree and act like a nut)

20. Where does a sheep go to get a haircut?
    (To the baa baa shop)

Tricky Riddles

21. How much dirt is in a hole six feet long by thirteen feet wide?
    (None. A hole is empty.)

22. Which weighs more: a pound of lead or a pound of feathers?
    (They both weigh a pound.)

23. What color was Washington's white horse?
    (White)

24. Who can jump higher than a tall building?
    (Anyone can. Tall buildings can't jump.)

More Jokes

25. A penny and a dollar were on a table. The penny jumped off. Why
    didn't the dollar?
    (The dollar had more sense.)

26. What do you call a rooster that doesn't crow?
    (Cock a doodle don't.)

27. What animal can fly higher than a house?
    (All of them...houses can't fly.)

28. Why did Sam take a ruler to bed
    with him?
    (So he could see how long he slept.)

29. What has an arm but cannot raise it?
    (A chair)

30. What has a big mouth but cannot talk?
    (A jar)

Knock Knock Jokes

Laughter creates a bond between people. Knock-knock jokes are delightful, fun ways to develop social skills because they require more than one person to play the game. As children grow and their social world expands, they will use the link of silliness and laughter to solidify their friendships.

1. Knock Knock
   Who's there?
   Dwayne
   Dwayne who?
   Dwayne the bathtub, I'm
   drowning!

2. Knock Knock
   Who's there?
   Amos
   Amos who?
   A mosquito bit me!

3. Knock Knock
   Who's there?
   Dishes
   Dishes who?
   Dishes the song that never
   ends!

4. Knock Knock
   Who's there?
   Boo
   Boo who?
   Why are you crying?

5. Knock Knock
   Who's there?
   Justin
   Justin who?
   Just in time for dinner!

6. Knock Knock
   Who's there?
   Wendy
   Wendy who?
   Wendy last time you took a
   bath?

7. Knock Knock
   Who's there?
   Abby
   Abby who?
   Abby birthday to you!!

8. Knock Knock
   Who's there?
   Eileen
   Eileen who?
   Eileen this way, and you lean
   that way!

9. Knock Knock
   Who's there?
   Gladys
   Gladys who?
   Gladys sunny outside today!

10. Knock Knock
    Who's there?
    Avenue
    Avenue who?
    Avenue heard this joke before?

11. Knock Knock
    Who's there?
    Sarah
    Sarah who?
    Sarah a doctor in the house?

12. Knock Knock
    Who's there?
    Atch
    Atch who?
    God bless you, that's a bad
       sneeze you have there!

13. Knock Knock
    Who's there?
    Sarah
    Sarah who?
    Sarah good movie on TV tonight?

14. Knock Knock
    Who's there?
    Oliver
    Oliver who?
    Oliver friends are coming over for a party!

15. Knock Knock
    Who's there?
    Isabel
    Isabel who?
    Isabel out of order? I had to knock!

16. Knock Knock
    Who's there?
    Hoppy
    Hoppy who?
    Hoppy Birthday to you!

17. Knock Knock
    Who's there?
    Radio
    Radio who?
    Radio not, here I come!

18. Knock Knock
    Who's there?
    Little Old Lady
    Little Old Lady who?
    Where did you learn to yodel?

19. Knock Knock
    Who's there?
    Doris
    Doris who?
    Doris locked—that's why I'm
        knocking!

20. Knock Knock
    Who's there?
    Noah
    Noah who?
    Noah good place to eat?

21. Knock Knock
    Who's there?
    Wanda
    Wanda who?
    Wanda go for a ride on
        my bike?

22. Knock Knock
    Who's there?
    Harry
    Harry who?
    Harry up and answer the
        door!

23. Knock Knock
    Who's there?
    Wayne
    Wayne who?
    Wayne Wayne go away

24. Knock Knock
    Who's there?
    Olive
    Olive who?
    Olive right next door to you!

25. Knock Knock
    Who's there?
    Howard
    Howard who?
    Howard was your lunch today?

26. Knock Knock
    Who's there?
    Scott
    Scott who?
    Scott nothing to do with you!

27. Knock Knock
    Who's there?
    Cargo
    Cargo who?
    Cargo beep beep

28. Knock Knock
    Who's there?
    Rain
    Rain who?
    Rain dear, you know, Rudolph
        the red-nosed rain dear!

29. Knock Knock
    Who's there?
    Ringo
    Ringo who?
    Ringo round the rosie!

30. Knock Knock
    Who's there?
    Rocky
    Rocky who?
    Rocky bye baby on the
        treetop!

31. Knock knock
    Who's there?
    Cows go
    Cows go who?
    No, silly. Cows go
        MOOOOOO!

Silly Songs and Books*

Read these books or sing these songs any time… they will make your body smile.

Dad's Dinosaur Day by Diane Dawson Hearn. Simon and Schuster, 1993. 0027434850. 32 pages.

Exaggerated, comic illustrations enhance this story about Mikey's father who turns into a dinosaur one morning. Mikey loves having a dinosaur dad when Dad takes him to school on his back, plays with the kids at recess, and takes a shower in the yard. But by the end of the day, Mikey wants his regular dad back.

Five Little Monkeys Jumping on the Bed by Eileen Christelow. Board book. Houghton Mifflin, 1998. 0395900239. 28 pages.

Gleeful, goofy monkeys start jumping on the bed as soon as they say good night to Mama. One by one, they fall off and hurt themselves. This happy, familiar rhyming story doubles as a counting book.

Good Thing You're Not an Octopus by Julie Marks. Illustrated by Maggie Smith. HarperCollins, 2001. 006028465X. 40 pages.

Young children will identify with the challenging activities of everyday life, such as being forced to eat lunch, climbing into the car seat, and taking a bath. But the narrator uses inventive psychology to make life seem more palatable. After all, "if you don't like to get dressed in the morning, it's a good thing you're not an octopus. If you were an octopus, you would have eight legs to put in your pants."

I Know an Old Lady Who Swallowed a Fly by Nadine Westcott. Little, Brown, and Co., 2003. 0316930849. 11 pages.

This favorite song about the old lady who keeps swallowing animals is humorously illustrated.

King Bidgood's in the Bathtub by Audrey Wood. Illustrated by Don Wood. Harcourt, 1985. 0152427309. 32 pages.

Magnificent illustrations are the highlight of this absurd, rhymed story about a king who refuses to get out of the bathtub and attend to his duties. Instead of persuading him to leave the tub, his court officials wind up in the tub with him. It is the young page who comes up with the obvious solution of pulling the plug.

* If you are unable to find one of these books in a bookstore, look for it at your local library.

The Lady With the Alligator Purse by Nadine Bernard Westcott. Board
Book. Little, Brown & Co., 1998. 0316930741. 24 pages.
This hilarious song, in which people come to help the ailing Tiny
Tim, has been a favorite for years.

Little Pig, Biddle Pig (Biddle Books) by David Kirk. Callaway Editions,
2001. 0439305756. 32 pages.
From the creator of the Miss Spider books comes this delightful story
of Little Pig, who is too fastidious to muck about in the mud. Each
page shows either primly pink Little Pig and other clean critters or
the gleeful "wiggly wallowers."

Miss Mary Mack: Sing-Along Stories by Mary Ann Hoberman. Illustrated
by Nadine Bernard Westcott. Little, Brown & Co., 2003. 0316076147.
32 pages.
The sheer silliness of the cartoon-like illustrations will appeal to
children who will delight in chanting along with the rhythmic,
repetitive humorous beat: "Miss Mary Mack, Mack, Mack/All dressed
in black, black, black."

Mr. Gumpy's Motor Car by John Burningham. HarperCollins Juvenile
Books, 1993. 069000799X. 32 pages.
Kind, patient Mr. Gumpy decides to go for a ride in the country, so
the children and farm animals beg to go along. When the car gets
stuck, they all have an excuse for not helping to push it out. They
finally cooperate, get the car out of the mud, and go for a pleasant
swim.

Mrs. Wishy-Washy by Joy Cowley. Illustrated by Elizabeth Fuller. Board
Book. Philomel, 1999. 0399233911. 16 pages.
Cow, Pig, and Duck are having a lovely time playing in the mud, but
when Mrs. Wishy-Washy sees them, she insists on getting them clean:
"wishy-washy, wishy-washy." Needless to say, as soon as she turns her
back, the animals are back in the mud. Great fun as a flannel board
story.

Mucky Moose by Jonathan Allen. Aladdin Library, 1996. 0689806515. 32 pages.
Mucky Moose loves to muck about in smelly swamps, which render
him truly "rotten-egg-old-sneaker" stinky. When the mean wolf
decides to eat Mucky, the odor overcomes him. Hilariously expressive
illustrations enhance the fun.

Mud by Mary Lyn Ray. Illustrated by Lauren Stringer. Voyager Books, 2001. 0152024611. 32 pages.
As spring comes, the winter frost thaws to become "gooey, gloppy, mucky, magnificent" mud. Children will easily identify with the young child's exhilaration of wallowing in the mud.

The Napping House by Audrey Wood. Illustrated by Don Wood. Board Book. Red Wagon Books, 2000. 0152026320. 16 pages.
Rhythmic, repetitive text relates the humorous story of everyone (granny, child, dog, cat, mouse) piling on top of each other to happily snooze in Granny's bed until a wakeful flea comes along.

No, David by David Shannon. Scholastic, 1998. 0590930028. 32 pages.
This autobiographical memoir strikes a chord with many a preschooler. David hears nothing but "No," from his mother as he writes on the wall, runs naked down the street, lets water overflow in the tub, and sticks his finger far up his nose.

Pig, Pigger, Piggest by Rick Walton. Illustrated by Jimmy Holder. Gibbs Smith, 1997. 0879058064. 32 pages.
The three pigs build castles that three witches blow down. The pigs are delighted with the mud holes that remain and ask the witch sisters to marry them.

The Piggy in the Puddle by Charlotte Pomerantz. Illustrated by James Marshall. Aladdin Library, 1989. 0689712936. 32 pages.
Hilarious, rhymed nonsense verses tell about members of a pig family who each leap with joyous abandon into a puddle.

Pigs in the Mud in the Middle of the Rud by Lynn Plourde. Illustrated by John Schoenherr. Scholastic, 1997. 0590568639. 32 pages.
When a family goes for a ride in their Model T, the road ("rud," as they say in rural Maine) is blocked by big pink pigs. To make matters worse, the pigs are joined by chickens, sheep, and bulls. The rollicking, rhyming, rhythmic text and exuberant illustrations create an uproariously fun storytime.

Roll Over! A Counting Song by Merle Peek. Houghton Mifflin, 1999. 0395957540. 32 pages.
This delightful song goes from 10 to 1, as the friendly animals roll over (and off) to make room for each other in bed.

Shake My Sillies Out by Raffi. Crown Publishing Group. 0517566478. 32 pages.
This is a great song to help children get all those wiggles out.

Sheep in a Jeep by Nancy Shaw. Illustrated by Margot Apple. Board Book. Houghton Mifflin, 1997. 039586786X. 26 pages.
Everything goes wrong when a flock of hapless sheep take a road trip through the country. The rhythm and rhyme and the ridiculous predicaments make this a terrific book to tickle your preschool storytime group: "Jeep goes splash! Jeep goes thud! Jeep goes deep in the gooey mud!"

Ten, Nine, Eight by Molly Bang. Board Book. Greenwillow, 1998. 0688149014. 24 pages.
Numbers from 10 to 1 are part of this lullaby that the little girl's father sings to her as she goes to bed.

This Old Man by Carol Jones. Houghton Mifflin, 1998. 0395901243. 42 pages.
This clever, witty peep-through-the-hole book, depicting the travels of "this old man" and his young companion, is filled with action and humor.

Today I Feel Silly and Other Moods That Make My Day by Jamie Lee Curtis. Illustrated by Laura Cornell. Joanna Cotler, 1998. 0060245603. 40 pages.
In this humorous rhyming book, a volatile frizzy-haired little girl describes 13 different feelings from silly to grumpy. The watercolor illustrations are wildly expressive and energetic, with a mood wheel on the last page that children can manipulate.

What Dads Can't Do by Douglas Wood. Illustrated by Doug Cushman. Simon & Schuster, 2000. 0689826206. 32 pages.
A young child-dinosaur describes what his single-parent father cannot do. He can't cross the street without holding hands; he can push, but he can't swing; and he really needs to be kissed goodnight at bedtime.

What Moms Can't Do by Douglas Wood. Illustrated by Doug Cushman. Simon & Schuster, 2001. 068983358. 32 pages.
These moms are dinosaurs, but they are incredibly similar to humans. The things that the mothers cannot do are obviously and humorously from a child's point of view: "Moms don't know how to keep salamanders in their shirts."

For Older Children

The Accidental Zucchini by Max Grover. Voyager Books, 1999.
0152015450. 36 pages.
This playful, rhythmic alphabet book will delight children ages 7-9
with its zany, new-wave illustrations of surreal urban scenes. Octopus
overalls dance on clotheslines, a vegetable volcano erupts carrots and
corn at skyscrapers, and a bathtub boat chugs down the river. Have
children make up their own fantasy worlds in words and pictures.

Clarice Bean, Guess Who's Babysitting? by Lauren Child. Candlewick
Press, 2001. 0763613738. 32 pages.
Firefighter Uncle Ted ends up babysitting Clarice and her siblings.
Chaos inevitably erupts with Minal on the way to the emergency
room and Grandfather wandering off to the neighbor's house.
Appealing cut-paper and photograph collages accent the hilarity.

Clarice Bean, That's Me by Lauren Child. Candlewick Press, 1999.
0763609617. 32 pages.
This wacky story about a madcap, melodramatic family is told from
the point of view of Clarice, who just wants some peace and quiet.
But with a pesky younger brother, an angst-filled older brother, a
boy-crazy sister, and other irritating relatives, she's not likely to get it.
The unconventional format of the book with a variety of fonts and
collages matches the chaos of the household.

Diane Goode's Book of Silly Stories and Songs edited by Adrienne Betz and
Lucia Monfried. Illustrated by Diane Goode. Dutton Books, 1992.
0525449671. 64 pages.
A hilarious collection of tall tales, folktales, and songs about the
antics of silly characters from around the world.

Ding Dong Ding Dong by Margie Palatini. Illustrated by Howard Fine.
Hyperion, 1999. 0786804203. 32 pages.
Children who are old enough to understand the cultural and
commercial references will find this spoof on King Kong, who is
selling Ape-On cosmetics door-to-door, hilarious. Fine's clever
illustrations with rich pastels and angled perspectives enhance the
humor.

Franny B. Kranny, There's a Bird in Your Hair! by Harriet Lerner and Susan Goldhor. Illustrated by Helen Oxenbury. HarperCollins, 2001. 0060246839. 40 pages.

Franny loves her long, frizzy red hair. She finally submits to letting a hairdresser style it. When a bird lands in Franny's hair, she is the hit of the family party, so she decides that putting her hair in rollers is okay.

Piggie Pie by Margie Palatini. Illustrated by Howard Fine. Clarion,1995. 0395716918. 32 pages.

This delightful, whimsical story about a witch who wants to make pork pie out of Old MacDonald's pigs has appeal far beyond the typical Halloween story. The author incorporates allusions to well-known stories and songs, such as *The Wizard of Oz* and *The Three Little Pigs,* as well as "Old MacDonald Had a Farm." Kids will get a chuckle out of clever dialogue: "I've been quack-quacked here and moo-mooed there, and cluck-clucked everywhere all over this farm."

The Scrambled States of America by Laurie Keller. Henry Holt & Co., 1998. 0805058028. 40 pages.

When Kansas wakes up bored and grumpy because it just sits there in the middle of the nation and never does anything interesting, he decides to throw a party. The states all end up trading places with hilariously unfortunate results.

The Stupids Step Out by Harry Allard. Illustrated by James Marshall. Houghton Mifflin, 1974. 0395185130. 32 pages.

The Stupid family and their dog, Kitty, do ridiculous things that allow young listeners to feel smugly superior.

The Stupids Take Off by Harry Allard. Illustrated by James Marshall. Houghton Mifflin, 1989. 0395500680. 32 pages.

The Stupids take off in a plane to avoid boring Uncle Carbuncle's visit. But they end up meeting more irritating relatives.

There Is a Carrot in My Ear: And Other Noodle Tales (I Can Read) by Alvin Schwartz. Photographs by Karen Ann Weinhaus. HarperCollins, 1982. 0060252340. 64 pages.

Six funny stories about a family of very silly people. Funny to read aloud as well as alone.

The Three Sillies by Walter J. De La Mare. Creative Education, 1993.
0886824672. 30 pages.
A young man believes his sweetheart and her family are the silliest
people in the world until he meets three others who are even sillier.
This is a classic traditional tale.

The Tickle Octopus by Audrey Wood. Illustrated by Don Wood. Harcourt,
1994. 0152008993. 46 pages.
Kids will be tickled by this clever story set in prehistoric times about
a pink octopus, who tickles members of a cave family, causing the
first smile, the first laughter, and the very first playing. The die-cut
pages and flimsy cardboard cover make it unsuitable for library
circulation, but you may want a copy to share at storytime. Use a
pink boa to tickle the children.

What Is a Wise Bird Like You Doing in a Silly Tale Like This? by Uri
Shulevitz. Farrar Straus & Giroux, 2000. 0374383006. 40 pages.
Three stories merge into one in this nonsense story about the
Emperor of Pickleberry who keeps a genius of a bird named Lou in a
cage. The fascinating collage illustrations are brilliant. The absurd
text, full of imaginary words, will stretch the imaginations of young
readers.

Whingdingdilly by Bill Peet. Houghton Mifflin, 1977. 0395247292. 64 pages.
Scamp learns to be content with his dog's life when Zildy the kooky
witch turns him into a Whingdingdilly. This humorous fantasy is
illustrated with comical crayon drawings.

The Wizard, the Fairy, and the Magic Chicken by Helen Lester. Illustrated
by Lynn Munsinger. Houghton Mifflin, 1983. 0395338859. 32 pages.
The three magic-making characters, including a chicken in a tutu,
compete against each other until they must learn to cooperate. This
terrifically clever book is great for storytime. Use props to augment
the fun.

Wizzil by William Steig. Illustrated by Quentin Blake. Farrar Straus and
Giroux, 2000. 0374384665. 32 pages.
Wizzil the witch is bored stiff until her parrot comes up with the idea
of tormenting farmer DeWitt Frimp. So Wizzil transmogrifies herself
into a housefly and is outraged when DeWitt swats her with a fly
swatter. The goofy plot thickens and twists from there with Wizzil
changing into a glove and ending up in the river where all her
nastiness washes away. DeWitt rescues her when she begins to drown

and they fall in love, marry, and live happily ever after. The silly, romantic story is perfectly illustrated with Blake's scratchy, comical illustrations.

Zoom Broom by Margie Palatini. Illustrated by Howard Fine. Hyperion Press, 2000. 0786814675. 32 pages.
Gritch the Witch is on the search for food again in this sequel to *Piggie Pie.* This time she wants to eat a nice filling, furry bunny rabbit. On her way to Farmer in the Dell's, her broomstick crashes and she is forced to buy a new vehicle at Foxy's used vehicle lot.

Language Games and Activities

Chapter 3

LEARNING POWER!

Children will laugh their way to learning about the following skills/concepts:

Body awareness
Cognitive thinking
Coordination
Creative movement
Creativity/Imagination
Dramatic play
Emotions
Empathy
Eye-hand coordination
Letter recognition
Listening
Observation
Phonemic awareness
Rhyming
Rhythm
Sequencing
Socialization
Vocabulary

Researchers at the University of Helsinki have proven that even before children are born, they begin to differentiate and memorize spoken sounds. From birth on, the running commentary that adults use as they care for children provides the foundation for language development in the preschool years. Playing with language is fun and educational. This chapter is full of games and activities that focus on words that are fun to say and play with. Children delight in renaming objects, creating new words with silly endings, and rhyming real and nonsense words. It all adds up to wonderful pre-reading and language skills.

Crickle, Crackle

1. The following poem is a wonderful introduction for a discussion about the wintertime, sounds, and weather.

Crickle, Crackle
When it is wintertime (hug yourself and shiver)
I run up the street (run in place)
And I make the ice laugh (laugh out loud)
With my little feet. (point to your feet)
"Crickle, crackle, crickle (step feet alternately on each word)
Crrrreet, crreet, creet." (scrape your feet heavily on the floor)

2. Try changing the initial sound of "Crickle, crackle, crickle," for even more giggles!

Diddle Diddle Dumpling

1. Say the following poem.

Diddle Diddle Dumpling
Diddle diddle dumpling
My son John
Went to bed with his stockings on.
One shoe off,
And one shoe on,
Diddle, diddle, dumpling
My son John.

2. Explain that the word "dumpling" is a term of affection, such as "honey," "sweetie," and "pumpkin."
3. Now, say the poem again with the children.
4. Say the poem with different beginning consonants. For example, say, "Biddle, biddle, bumpling…" or "Ziddle, ziddle, zumpling…".

Copy Cats

1. Choose a favorite nursery rhyme or poem and say the first line in a silly voice. For example:

   Humpty Dumpty sat on a wall (say in a silly voice)

2. Ask the group to finish the rhyme and copy your voice.
3. Try speaking in other voices, such as a high, low, fast, slow, whiny, whispering, happy, sad, or nasal voice.

> **LEARNING POWER!**
>
> **Children will laugh their way to learning about the following skills/concepts:**
>
> Creativity/Imagination
> Listening

I Saw a Bear

1. Teach the following in a call-and-response manner.

   Adult: *The other day*
   Child: *The other day*
   Adult: *I saw a bear*
   Child: *I saw a bear*
   Adult: *A great big bear*
   Child: *A great big bear*
   Adult: *Away up there.*
   Child: *Away up there.*
   Together: *The other day I saw a bear. A great big bear away up there.*

2. Continue, saying each line and then repeating it together.

   He looked at me
   I looked at him
   He sized up me
   I sized up him.
   Together…

   And so I ran
   Away from there
   And right behind me
   Was that bear.
   Together…

> **LEARNING POWER!**
>
> **Children will laugh their way to learning about the following skills/concepts:**
>
> Listening
> Sequencing

In front of me
There was a tree
A great big tree
Oh, golly gee.
Together…

The nearest branch
Was ten feet up
I had to jump
And trust my luck.
Together…

And so I jumped
Into the air
And missed that branch
Away up there.
Together…

Now don't you fret
And don't you frown
I caught that branch
On the way back down.
Together…

That's all there is
There is no more
Unless I meet
That bear once more.
Together…

3. Let the children take turns being the bear and acting out the poem.

4. As you act out the poem, keep asking, "What comes next?"

LEARNING POWER!

Children will laugh their way to learning about the following skills/concepts:

Rhyming

The Cuckoo

1. Enjoy this playful rhyme together. Encourage the children to sing in their best "bird" voices and then fly away.

The Cuckoo
Cuckoo, cuckoo,
What do you do?
In April
I open my bill.
In May
I sing night and day.
In June
I change my tune.
In July
Away I fly.

Itchy Flea

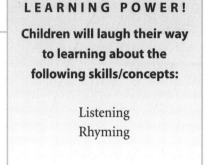

1. Teach the following in a call-and-response manner.

    Adult: *Flea*
    Child: *Flea*
    Adult: *Flea fly*
    Child: *Flea fly*
    Adult: *Flea fly mosquito*
    Child: *Flea fly mosquito*
    Adult: *Oh no, no, no more mosquitoes*
    Child: *Oh no, no, no more mosquitoes*
    Adult: *Itchy itchy, scratchy scratchy, oh I got one down my backy!*
    Child: *Itchy itchy, scratchy scratchy, oh I got one down my backy!*
    Adult: *Beat that big bad bug with the bug spray!*
    Child: *Beat that big bad bug with the bug spray!*
    Everyone: *Shhh!*

2. Use different vocal inflections on each line. For example, say the word "mosquito" in a high, squeaky voice or say the last line in a low, deep voice.

Silly Singing

1. Choose a familiar song and change the words to something silly.
2. For example, sing "Yankee Doodle" and change "macaroni" to "pizza" or "ice cream."
3. Other ideas include:

    ★ Sing "Skip to My Lou" and change "flies in the buttermilk" to another insect and something else to drink, such as "ants in the orange juice."
    ★ Sing "Twinkle, Twinkle, Little Star..." and ask what else could twinkle, such as snow, the moon, or a lightning bug.

4. Make up new verses. Ask for suggestions.

My Dame Has a Lame Tame Crane

1. Say the following poem. Children will enjoy the way the words sound, and they will learn about vowel sounds at the same time.

My dame has a lame tame crane.
My dame has a crane that is lame.
Pray, gentle Jane, let my crane that is lame
Eat, and come home again.

2. Say the poem and substitute another long vowel with the "a" words. For example:

My deem has a leem teem creen…
My dime has a lime time crine…
My dome has a lome tome crone…
My dume has a lume tume crune…

3. This gets to be pretty silly and lots of fun!

There Was a Bee-Eye-Ee-Eye-Ee

1. Practicing vowel sounds has never been this much fun!

There was a bee eye ee eye ee
Sat on a wall eye all eye all
And there he sat eye at eye at
And that was all eye all eye all

Then came a boy eye oy eye oy
Who had a stick eye ick eye ick
And gave that bee eye ee eye ee
An awful lick eye ick eye ick.

And so that bee eye ee eye ee
Began to sting eye ing eye ing
And hurt that boy eye oy eye oy
Like anything eye ing eye ing.

And then that bee eye ee eye ee
Gave one big cough eye off eye off
And one last smile eye ile eye ile
And he buzzed off eye off eye off.

Fruit Game
(with or without props)

LEARNING POWER!

Children will laugh their way to learning about the following skills/concepts:

Creativity/Imagination
Listening

1. If you have fruit toys (manipulatives, erasers, toys), use them with this activity. Otherwise, use pictures of the different fruits. (Note: This activity works with or without props.) Children will learn about sound words.

2. Sing the following to the tune of "Have You Ever Seen a Lassie?" Hold up an apple and sing.

   Have you ever had an apple, an apple, an apple?
   Have you ever had an apple?
   And heard it go CRUNCH! (make a crunch, crunch sound)

3. Hold up an orange and sing.

   Have you ever had an orange, an orange, an orange?
   Have you ever had an orange?
   And heard it go SLURP! (make a slurping sound)

   Additional verses:
   Grapes go POP
   Bananas go MUSH
   Strawberries go MUNCH
   Lemons go OOO! (make a sour face)

Funny Name Sounds

LEARNING POWER!

Children will laugh their way to learning about the following skills/concepts:

Creativity/Imagination
Phonemic awareness
Rhyming

1. Pick a first or last name and say the first letter of the name. For example, "Jake begins with the letter 'J.'"
2. Ask how the name "Jake" would sound if it began with a different letter such as "C."
3. Continue with other letters.
4. Do the same thing with different categories of words, such as food, transportation, games, and so on. Children enjoy many laughs as they play this game.

Silly Willy

1. Sing the following words to the tune of "Skip to my Lou."

   Silly Willy, who should I choose?
   Silly Willy, who should I choose?
   Silly Willy, who should I choose?
   I choose _____.

2. Choose a name and rhyme it, for example, "Wacky Jackie" or "Goofy Ruthie."
3. Use this song to name friends, relatives, animal friends, and so on.
4. It's okay to use rhyming words that are made-up words, such as "Robert wobert…"

The Letter Walk

1. Put masking tape on the floor in the shape of a letter, such as "M."
2. Say the letter and think of all the "M" words that you can.
3. Point out distinctive things about the letter; in this case, the letter "M" has four straight lines.
4. Walk around the letter and sing the following words to "Mary Had a Little Lamb."

   Walk around the letter "M," letter "M," letter "M."
   Walk around the letter "M."
   Walk until you stop! (stop and freeze on the word "stop")

5. Continue with jumping, hopping, running, and other motions.
6. Change to another letter.
7. Ask the children for silly movement suggestions, such as "make a funny face," "shake your body as you move," or "shake your hands over your head as you move." Or suggest that when they step they can hiccup, laugh, or stick out their tongue.

Gibberish

1. Gibberish is a non-language. It's a lot of sounds that have no meaning so the meaning has to be expressed through intonation and body language.
2. Ask a question in gibberish. The response can be a shake of the heads either "yes" or "no" or more gibberish!
3. Encourage conversation in gibberish.
4. Young children love to play this game. They can make up any sounds that they wish as they talk in gibberish.

> **LEARNING POWER!**
>
> **Children will laugh their way to learning about the following skills/concepts:**
>
> Creativity/Imagination

Name Rhymes

1. Make up a rhyme for people you know. Even if the rhyming word doesn't make sense, listening to the rhyme will be fun.
2. Say this verse for each name.

What's your name?
Your name is Bill.
Bill, Bill walks up the hill.

What's your name?
Your name is Denise.
Denise, Denise, we wish you peace.

What's your name?
Your name is Jackie.
Jackie, Jackie, quacky, quacky.

3. Rhyme animal names, people in the neighborhood, and characters from books.

> **LEARNING POWER!**
>
> **Children will laugh their way to learning about the following skills/concepts:**
>
> Creativity/Imagination
> Rhyming

Changing Voices

1. Did you ever think about the many ways that you can make your voice sound? Changing the quality of the sound and the rhythm of words is an excellent way to develop language skills.

2. Pick a phrase such as, "Hip, Hip Hooray!" and say it in many different ways, including the following ideas:

   ★ Hold your nose as you talk.
   ★ Cup your hands around your mouth as you talk.
   ★ Say the phrase loudly.
   ★ Say the phrase softly.
   ★ Pucker your lips as you say the words.
   ★ Put your hand over your mouth as you say the words.

Pizza Pie

1. Make up actions to go with the words. On the "yum, yum" part, rub your tummy.

Pizza Pie
Give me a P
Give me an I
I've almost got my pizza pie.
Two more Zs and one more A,
We'll have a pizza pie today.
Here's the sauce,
Here's the cheese.
Would you pass the pizza, please!
Yum, yum, yum, yum!
—Jackie Silberg

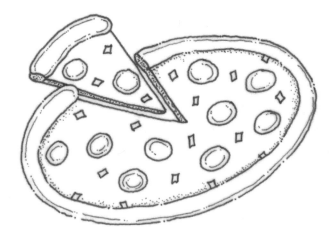

Nonsense Sentences

1. Sing the song "Oh, Susannah" and explain to the children how the words are silly and unexpected because, for example, the weather wouldn't be dry if it were raining.

   It rained so hard the day I left
   The weather it was dry.
   The sun so hot, I froze to death,
   Susannah don't you cry.

2. Make up nonsense sentences and ask what's funny about them. For example:

   ★   I put my bathing suit on to go ice-skating.
   ★   I ate my cereal from a glass.
   ★   I washed my hands with sugar.
   ★   I painted pictures with a hammer.

Three Craw

1. A little nonsense now and then is relished by the wisest men. The words in this poem are in Scottish dialect. They are easy to pronounce because of the rhyme scheme.

Three Craw
Three craw sat upon a wa, sat upon a wa, sat upon a wa
Three craw sat upon a wa
On a cold and frosty morning.

The first craw couldna find his maw, couldna find his maw, couldna
    find his maw
The first craw couldna find his maw,
On a cold and frosty morning.

The second craw couldna find his paw
The third craw ate the other twa
The fourth craw warna there at aw
And that's aw I hear about the craw.

2. Change the words to reflect different vowel sounds, such as:

Three cray sat upon a way…
Three crow sat upon a wo…
Three cree sat upon a wee…

LEARNING POWER!

Children will laugh their way to learning about the following skills/concepts:

Rhyming

Moses Supposes His Toeses Are Roses

1. Ask the children to repeat each line of the poem after you say it.

Moses Supposes His Toeses Are Roses
Moses supposes his toeses are roses,
But Moses supposes erroneously.
For nobody's toeses we knowes are roses,
As Moses supposes his toeses to be!

2. Repeat the rhyming words: "Moses," "supposes," "toeses," and "roses."
3. Repeat, clapping on each "o" sound. The rhythm of the rhyme is such that a long "o" sound falls on each beat. After mastering clapping, add stomping feet on each long "o."
4. Come up with other words to rhyme with Moses. They can be real words or made-up words, such as "dozes," "blowses," or "growses."

See You Later, Alligator

1. Use these funny sayings whenever you want to make someone laugh and smile.

   See you later, alligator.
   In a while, crocodile.

   See you later, hot potato.
   If you wish, jellyfish!

   Not too soon, you big baboon.
   Toodle-oo, kangaroo.

2. Make up some of your own.

Story Listening

1. Record a story using a tape recorder. When you record the story, let the children add the sound effects as you record or make sound effects yourself. Children find this very humorous.
2. Choose a story that lends itself to plenty of sound effects, such as:

   ★ *Mr. Brown Can Moo, Can You?* by Dr. Seuss
   ★ *Good Night, Owl* by Pat Hutchins
   ★ *Too Much Noise* by Ann McGovern

3. Choose stories that have questions in the text ("What should the wide-mouthed frog do to get away from the alligator?" in *The Wide-Mouthed Frog* by Keith Faulkner) and record the answers on the tape.
4. Put the tape and a copy of the book together in a zipper-closure plastic bag to make your own audiobook set.
5. Children will love reading the book and listening to the tape.

Down by the Bay

LEARNING POWER!

Children will laugh their way to learning about the following skills/concepts:

Rhyming

1. Repeat each line except the last line.

   Down by the bay,
   Down by the bay,

   Where the watermelons grow,
   Where the watermelons grow,

   Back to my home,
   Back to my home,

   I dare not go.
   I dare not go.

   For if I do,
   For if I do,

   My mother will say,
   My mother will say,

   "Did you ever see a cow with a green eyebrow
   Down by the bay?"

2. Make up rhyming words for the last line, such as:

   Did you ever see a horse on a golf course?
   Did you ever see a snake baking a cake?
   Did you ever see a pig dancing a jig?
   Did you ever see a bear combing his hair?
   Did you ever see a carp playing the harp?

Dirty Bill

1. Although this is a silly song/rhyme, it is a great opportunity to talk about the importance of cleanliness.

   I know a man named Dirty Bill
   He lives in a house on garbage hill
   Never took a bath and never will
   Yuk! Yuk! Dirty Bill.

2. Talk about good hygiene habits such as taking a bath each day, washing your hands and hair, and brushing your teeth.
3. If you don't know the melody of this song, you can say it as a rhyme.

> **LEARNING POWER!**
>
> **Children will laugh their way to learning about the following skills/concepts:**
>
> Body awareness
> Rhyming
> Socialization

Today Is Monday

1. Sequencing is a very important pre-reading skill. To teach this concept in a fun way, chant the following humorous cumulative rhyme. By the time you get near the end, the children will have fun trying to remember the correct sequence.

> **LEARNING POWER!**
>
> **Children will laugh their way to learning about the following skills/concepts:**
>
> Sequencing

Today Is Monday
Today is Monday,
Today is Monday,
Monday spaghetti
All you hungry children
Come and eat it up.

Today is Tuesday,
Today is Tuesday,
Tuesday string beans,
Monday spaghetti,
All you hungry children
Come and eat it up.

Today is Wednesday,
Today is Wednesday,
Wednesday soup,
Tuesday string beans,
Monday spaghetti,
All you hungry children
Come and eat it up.

Today is Thursday,
Today is Thursday,
Thursday roast beef,
Wednesday soup,
Tuesday string beans,
Monday spaghetti,
All you hungry children
Come and eat it up.

Today is Friday,
Today is Friday,
Friday fish,
Thursday roast beef,
Wednesday soup,
Tuesday string beans,
Monday spaghetti,
All you hungry children
Come and eat it up.

Today is Saturday,
Today is Saturday,
Saturday payday,
Friday fish,
Thursday roast beef,
Wednesday soup,
Tuesday string beans,
Monday spaghetti,
All you hungry children
Come and eat it up.

Today is Sunday,
Today is Sunday,
Sunday church,
Saturday payday,
Friday fish,
Thursday roast beef,
Wednesday soup,
Tuesday string beans,
Monday spaghetti,
All you hungry children
Come and eat it up.

2. This rhyme is easily adaptable to other time-oriented concepts, such as the seasons of the year or the hours of the day. Use your imagination!

LEARNING POWER!

Children will laugh their way to learning about the following skills/concepts:

Creativity/Imagination
Dramatic play
Listening
Rhyming

The Princess Pat

1. This is a repetition song—the leader speaks a line and children repeat it. Say each line, and ask the children to repeat it.

The Princess Pat
The Princess Pat
The Princess Pat
Lived in a tree
Lived in a tree
She sailed across
She sailed across
The seven seas
The seven seas.

2. Continue the rhyme, with the children repeating each line after you.

But her ship sank
And yours will too
If you don't take
A rickadandoo.

A rickadandoo
Now what is that?
It's something made
By the Princess Pat.
It's red and gold
And purple, too.
That's why it's called
A rickadandoo.

Now Captain Jack
Had a mighty fine crew.
They sailed across
The channel, too.
But his ship sank
And yours will, too
If you don't take
A rickadandoo.

A rickadandoo
Now what is that?
It's something made
By the Princess Pat.
It's red and gold
And purple, too.
That's why it's called
A rickadandoo!

DID YOU KNOW?

Here is the true meaning behind Princess Pat: "Princess Patricia's Light Infantry" is part of the Royal Canadian Legion, which distinguished itself in two world wars and remains part of Canada's armed forces today.

The "Rickadandoo" is a nickname for the infantry's red, gold, and purple regimental flag. Princess Patricia of Connaught is the daughter of a Governor General of Canada (1911–1914) and granddaughter of Queen Victoria and Prince Albert.

And now, the true lyrics:

The Princess Pat's Light Infantry
They sailed across the seven seas
They sailed across the channel too
And they took with them, the Rickadandoo.

Chorus:
The Rickadandoo, now what is that?
It's something made by the Princess Pat
It's red and gold, and purple too,
That's why it's called, the Rickadandoo.

Now Captain Jack, had a mightily fine crew,
They sailed across the channel too,
But his ship sank, and yours will too,
If you don't take the Rickadandoo.

Chorus

The Princess Pat, saw Captain Jack,
She reeled him in, and brought him back,
She saved his life, and his crew's too,
And do you know how?—with the Rickadandoo.

Chorus

Bubble Gum

1. Use the following silly song to start a discussion about money.

My mom gave me a penny.
She said, "Go talk to Kenny."
But I didn't talk to Kenny,
Instead I bought some bubble gum.

Chorus:
Bazooka, zooka bubble gum
Bazooka, bubble gum
Bazooka zooka bubble gum
Bazooka bubble gum!

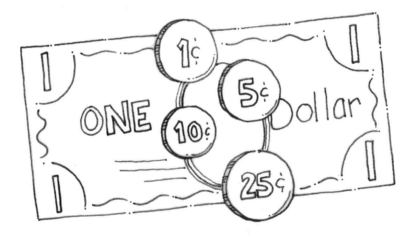

My mom gave me a nickel.
She said, "Go buy a pickle."
But I didn't buy a pickle,
Instead I bought some bubble gum.

Chorus

My mom gave me a dime.
She said, "Go buy a lime."
But I didn't buy a lime,
Instead I bought some bubble gum.

Chorus

My mom gave me a quarter.
She said, "Go buy some water."
But I didn't buy some water,
Instead I bought some bubble gum.

Chorus

My mom gave me a dollar.
She said, "Go buy a collar."
But I didn't buy a collar,
Instead I bought some bubble gum.

Chorus

Old John Muddlecombe

> **LEARNING POWER!**
>
> **Children will laugh their way to learning about the following skills/concepts:**
>
> Rhyming

1. Say the following humorous rhyme together.

Old John Muddlecombe
Old John Muddlecombe lost his cap.
He couldn't find it anywhere, the poor old chap.
He walked down the High Street and everyone said,
"Silly John Muddlecombe, you've got it on your head."

Imagination Games and Activities

The following chapter contains games and activities that develop children's creativity and imagination. Stretching the imagination, thinking outside the box, and learning to look at a situation from different angles are all long-term benefits of this type of play. Child psychologist Niki Saros observes that children who are creative thinkers have a certain mental flexibility that allows them to escape from the pressure of a hyper-structured view of the world. That skill translates into creative problem solving in later years (*Home Extension Line Newsletter*, April 2001, Issue 3).

Creativity and imagination are wonderful traits for children to possess. By cultivating these two important skills, you teach children to be optimists, to see the possibilities where they might otherwise see barriers, and to have a sense of humor in the way they approach life. From imagining what else Old Mother Hubbard might go to the cupboard for, to imagining what a tiger might look like if it were a fish, this chapter encourages children to suspend reality and enjoy the humor in the outlandish. By doing so, children become creative storytellers, thinkers, dreamers, and doers.

To encourage children's creativity:

★ Provide an environment that lets children explore and play without unnecessary restraints.

★ Adapt children's ideas instead of trying to make their ideas fit yours.

★ Accept children's divergent problem solving without judgment.

★ Use your own creative problem solving to tackle everyday situations.

★ Allow children time to explore many possibilities in any given situation so they can create their own original solutions and ideas.

★ Emphasize the process rather than the product in children's activities.

Old Mother Hubbard

1. Say the following poem.

   Old Mother Hubbard went to the cupboard
   To get her poor dog a bone.
   When she got there
   The cupboard was bare
   And so her poor dog had none.

2. Change some of the words. "She went to the cupboard to get her poor dog a _____." Fill in with different words, such as "pizza," "dress," "hat," and so on.
3. Change the word "dog" to another animal: "to get her poor giraffe a cake" or "to get her poor hippopotamus a banana."
4. Ask the children to give you other ideas for animals and silly objects.

> **LEARNING POWER!**
>
> **Children will laugh their way to learning about the following skills/concepts:**
>
> Creativity/Imagination

There Is a Painted Bus

1. Say this rhyme, and then repeat it while doing the actions suggested below.

   There is a painted bus, (draw an imaginary bus with your arms)
   With twenty painted seats. (pretend to sit on a seat)
   It carries painted people (pretend to drive the bus)
   Along the painted streets.

   They pull the painted bell. (pretend to pull a bell chain)
   The painted driver stops, (pretend to put on the brakes)
   And they all get out (pretend to leave the bus)
   At the little painted shops.

2. Saying the rhyme faster encourages even more laughter from the children.
3. "The Wheels on the Bus" is a good song to sing with the poem.

> **LEARNING POWER!**
>
> **Children will laugh their way to learning about the following skills/concepts:**
>
> Body awareness
> Dramatic play
> Listening
> Rhyming

Ten Munching Monkeys

1. Say the following funny poem. The children will learn counting and rhyming skills, and tap into their own creativity and imagination. Use your fingers to indicate the numbers.

Ten Munching Monkeys

Ten munching monkeys
Came to school one day.
One found a carrot
And ran outside to play.

Oh, little monkey
Why did you go away?
Now we have nine monkeys
At our school today.

Nine munching monkeys—found a tomato
Eight munching monkeys—found an onion
Seven munching monkeys—found some celery
Six munching monkeys—found a potato
Five munching monkeys—found a parsnip
Four munching monkeys—found some parsley
Three munching monkeys—found some cabbage
Two munching monkeys—found some green beans

One munching monkey
Came to school one day.
He didn't find the others.
Did they run away?
The teacher said, "Let's go outside and see what we can find."
And when they found the others
What a wonderful surprise!
—Jackie Silberg

2. Ask the children to give you ideas about what they think the other monkeys were doing.

I Wish I Were

1. Teach the song and do the actions. Make up actions to go with the words in the second and third verses.

I Wish I Were
(Tune: "If You're Happy and You Know It")
Oh, I wish I were a little slice of orange. (pretend to peel an orange)
Oh, I wish I were a little slice of orange.
I'd go squirty, squirty, squirty
Over everybody's shirtie. (flick fingers and then rub hands on your shirt)
Oh, I wish I were a little slice of orange. (repeat actions for the first line)

Additional verses:
Oh, I wish I were a little mosquito.
Oh, I wish I were a little mosquito.
I'd go bitey, bitey, bitey
Over everybody's nightie.
Oh, I wish I were a little mosquito.

Oh, I wish I were a little lollipop.
Oh, I wish I were a little lollipop.
I would licky, licky, licky
'Til I'm nothing but a sticky.
Oh, I wish I were a little lollipop.

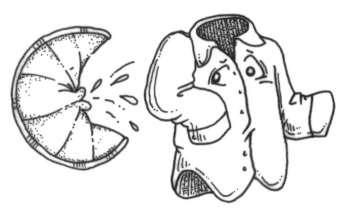

Gregory Griggs

1. Act out the following humorous rhyme.

Gregory Griggs
Gregory Griggs, Gregory Griggs
Had twenty-seven different wigs,
He wore them up, he wore them down
To please the people of the town.
He wore them east, he wore them west
But he never could tell which he liked the best.

2. Give the children paper and crayons or markers and suggest that they draw a wig that Gregory Griggs might wear.

Poor Little Bug on the Wall

1. Say the following chant with expression.

   Poor little bug on the wall,
   No one to love him at all.
   No one to wash his clothes,
   No one to tickle his toes,
   Poor little bug on the wall.

2. As a variation, talk like a baby:

   Poor wittle bug on the wall, WAH WAH
   No one to wuv him at all. WAH WAH
   No one to wash his clothes, WAH WAH
   No one to tickle his toes, WAH WAH
   Poor wittle bug on the wall. WAH WAH

3. Ask the children to draw pictures of a bug with clothes, toes, and so on. Ask questions such as, "How many toes does your bug have?" "What is your bug going to wear today?" This would make a great art project. Ask the children to name their bug and tell a story about why he has no one to love him at all. Encourage them to imagine how the bug might feel.

Imaginative Talking

1. Imagine what various objects in a room would say if they could talk. What would the flowers say? What would a chair say?
2. Suggest some and soon children will be making up their own ideas. Suggestions include:

   ★ What does the chair say? …"Please sit down on me backwards."
   ★ What does the flower say? …"May I have some water so I can brush my teeth?"

Yummy Cookies

1. Adapt the "Peanut…Peanut Butter" chant by changing it to "Cookies, Yummy Cookies" (see below for an example). Change the verses accordingly: "First you take the eggs and you break 'em, you break 'em" or "First you take the dough and you stir it, you stir it" (whatever level of detail you want to get into with the recipe is fine).

2. Work up to "You put 'em in the oven and you bake 'em, you bake 'em." Have some cookies already hidden within reach (the Housekeeping Area toy oven would be a neat place). When you say, "Then you take 'em out and you eat 'em, you eat 'em!" pull out the cookies from their hiding place! The kids will think you did a magic trick! And they will be thrilled to get to eat REAL cookies instead of pretend. They will probably ask you to do this magic trick every day.

Yummy Cookies
First you take the eggs and
you break 'em, you break 'em
break 'em, break 'em, break 'em.

Chorus:
Cookies, yummy cookies—eat 'em!
Cookies, yummy cookies—eat 'em!

Then you take the flour and
You measure, you measure,
Measure, measure, measure.

Chorus:
Cookies, yummy cookies—eat 'em!
Cookies, yummy cookies—eat 'em!

3. Continue as suggested above.

LEARNING POWER!

Children will laugh their way to learning about the following skills/concepts:

Body awareness
Creative movement
Creativity/Imagination
Listening
Sequencing
Socialization

Fish Is Fish... Or Is It?

1. Leo Lionni's book *Fish Is Fish* tells the story of a fish that imagines land animals but can't help imagining them with fins and tails!
2. Why not create more fishy imaginations? Here are some ideas.

   ★ Cut out a fishtail from construction paper, and attach it to the back of any toy animal.
   ★ Draw land animals and add fishy tails and scales to them.
   ★ Draw suggested animals with fishy tails and fins on the blackboard or chart paper.

3. Any way you do it, it's sure to be funny!

The Eccentric

1. Say the first line of each stanza. Together, say, "Oh, what an afternoon."

   The Eccentric
   He powdered his hair with pumpkin squash,
   Oh, what an afternoon!

   And sent his dirty teeth to the wash.
   Oh, what an afternoon!

   Oh what a, oh what a, oh what a, oh what a,
   Oh, what an afternoon!

2. Say the poem again and as you say, "Oh, what an afternoon," clap your hands at the same time.
3. Continue expressing the rhythm by stamping your feet.
4. Talk about the word "eccentric." Explain that the person in the poem is someone who does unusual things that most people wouldn't do.
5. Make up some fun ways to do things in a different way. For example, brushing your teeth while standing on one foot or getting dressed by putting on your shoes first.

Johnny Brown

1. Read the following poem.
2. Each line ends with a question. Encourage children to answer the question with the appropriate facial expression. For example, when you ask, "Can you frown like Johnny Brown?" ask children to answer by frowning.
3. There are many ways to frown, whimper, mope and smile. Demonstrate with the children before saying the poem.

Johnny Brown had a frown.
Can you frown like Johnny Brown?

Mary Crimper had a whimper.
Can you whimper like Mary Crimper?

Betty Hope had a mope.
Can you mope like Betty Hope?

But Lillian Lyle had a lovely smile.
Can you smile like Lillian Lyle?

When I Went Out

1. Say the following humorous rhyme together.

> *When I went out for a walk one day,*
> *My head fell off and rolled away,*
> *And when I saw that it was gone*
> *I picked it up and put it on.*
>
> *When I went into the street*
> *Someone shouted, "Look at your feet!"*
> *I looked at them and sadly said,*
> *"I've left them both asleep in bed."*

There Was an Old Man

1. Say the following humorous rhyme together.

> *There was an old man with a beard*
> *Who said, "It is just as I feared—*
> *Two owls and a hen, four larks and a wren*
> *Have all built their nests in my beard!"*
> —Edward Lear

2. Draw a large picture of a man with a beard. Ask the children what you could put in his beard. As the children make the suggestions, draw their ideas in the picture. You could also cut out magazine pictures of owls, hens, larks, and wrens, and let the children stick them on the beard.

I Eat My Peas With Honey

1. Show what the following rhyme means by putting some peas on a knife that is coated with honey. This is great fun!

I eat my peas with honey.
I've done it all my life.
It makes the peas taste funny,
But it keeps them on the knife.

Sam, Sam the Dirty Man

1. Say the following humorous rhyme together. Talk about different things the children could brush their hair or scratch their stomachs with.

   Sam, Sam, the dirty man
   Washed his face in a frying pan,
   Combed his hair with the back of a chair,
   And danced with a toothache in the air.

   Sam, Sam, the dirty man
   Washed his face in a frying pan,
   Brushed his hair with a donkey's tail
   And scratched his tummy with his big toenail.

Chapter 5

Active Games and Activities

This chapter is full of games and activities that address children's need to move. To make these games and activities even more enjoyable, show the children how to do an action in slow motion. Try clapping, walking, moving like different animals, running, sitting down, and walking backwards all in slow motion.

For young children, humor is often connected to ongoing play activities. Much of laughter is a release of excitement built up through physical activity. "Acting silly" enables children to demonstrate a mastery of physical skills. Running, jumping, or screaming can all be manifestations of children's sense of humor.

The Balloon Game

1. Give three or four inflated balloons to the group.
2. Play some music, such as "Up, Up, and Away," "Let's Go Fly a Kite," or "The Man on the Flying Trapeze."
3. Instruct the group to work together to keep the balloons in the air while the music is playing. When the music stops, they let the balloons float to the ground.
4. Now comes even more fun—stop the music and then start it again before the balloons reach the ground. The group must keep the balloons from reaching the floor.

Silly Obstacle Course Relay

1. Place four objects, such as a large box that is open at each end, a jump rope, a bicycle horn, and a beanbag chair, around the room.
2. Encourage one child at a time to go through the obstacle course as follows: crawl through the box, jump over the rope, honk the bicycle horn, sit in the beanbag chair, and then sit on the floor.

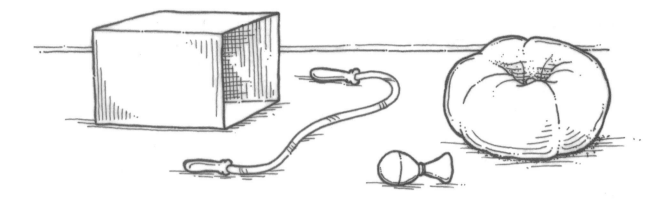

3. The next child proceeds through the obstacle course. Continue until each child has had a turn.

4. When everyone has finished, ask the group what they did first, second, third, and last.

5. Ask the children for silly ways they could go through the obstacle course, such as backwards, or while flapping their arms like a bird. They will be laughing and learning at the same time!

The Body Walk

1. Talk about walking and using two parts of your body.
2. How can you walk on three parts of your body? (two legs and one arm; two knees and one elbow)
3. Try walking on four parts of your body. (two knees and two elbows)
4. Explore all the different ways to walk on four parts.
5. Can they think of five parts? (slide sitting down with hands on the floor)

LEARNING POWER!

Children will laugh their way to learning about the following skills/concepts:

Body awareness
Coordination
Creative movement
Sequencing

Jelly in the Bowl

1. Act out the following rhyme with the children.

   Jelly in the bowl
   Jelly in the bowl
   Wibble wobble, wibble wobble
   Jelly in the bowl.

2. Change the words by thinking of other foods to substitute for jelly, such as:

   Cereal in the bowl
   Cereal in the bowl
   Crunchy, crunchy, crunchy, crunchy
   Cereal in the bowl.

   Oatmeal in the bowl
   Oatmeal in the bowl
   Gushy, smushy, gushy, smushy
   Oatmeal in the bowl.

Windy Reading

1. Instead of turning the pages of a book, blow them! Children will LOVE doing this!
2. *The Wind Blew* by Pat Hutchins is a perfect book to try this idea.
3. Other books you can try are:

   ★ *Gilberto and the Wind* by Marie Hall Ets
   ★ *Old Devil Wind* by Barry Root
   ★ *The Wind's Garden* by Bethany Roberts
   ★ *Wind Says Goodnight* by Katy Rydell

Popcorn Rhyme

1. Say the following rhyme and do the actions.

   Pop, pop, pop, (jump up from a squatting position)
   Pour the corn into the pot, (pretend to pour corn into a pot)
   Pop, pop, pop, (repeat popping actions)
   Take and shake it 'til it's hot. (shake your body)
   Pop, pop, pop, (repeat popping actions)
   Lift the lid and what have you got? (pretend to lift the lid)
   Popcorn! (jump up and down)

2. This fun rhyme can start a discussion about how a kernel changes into popcorn, and how when something gets hot, it becomes different, for example, water when it boils, butter or chocolate when it melts, and ice when it thaws.

3. Talk about popcorn. Popcorn is a type of corn with small, hard kernels. The kernels contain moisture, and, when they are heated, the heat changes the moisture to steam. The hard covering keeps the steam from escaping, causing pressure to build up inside the kernel. The pressure finally bursts the kernel, producing the white, starchy substance called popcorn.

4. Use a popcorn popper and watch popcorn pop!
   Note: Use appropriate caution and supervision when popping corn.

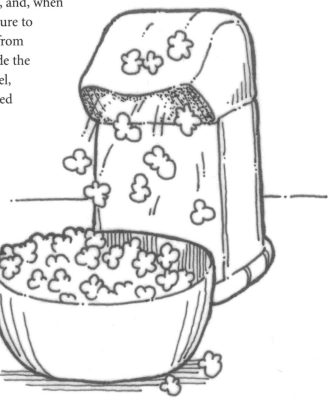

Bubble Poke and Hold

1. Bubbles and children are always a playful, fun combination!
2. Put a lot of bubble solution in a dishpan.
3. Blow bubbles.
4. Demonstrate that bubbles pop when touched.
5. Then put your hands in the bubble solution and touch the bubbles again. This time the bubbles will not pop.
6. Bubbles pop when something dry touches them (the dry object absorbs water and makes a hole). However, something wet (soapy wet is even better) can touch the wall of a bubble without creating a hole.
7. Encourage the children to run around and "catch" the bubbles. The sound of laughter and squeals of delight are sure to follow. They will learn about bubbles and have fun doing it.

I'm a Little Acorn Brown

1. Recite the rhyme "I'm a Little Acorn Brown" and act out each verse.
2. This is a good activity to talk about animal sounds and characteristics.
3. The third verse reveals information about frogs: they sit on logs, eat flies and bugs, and make a croaking noise.

I'm a Little Acorn Brown

I'm a little acorn brown,
Living on the cold, cold ground.
Everybody steps on me
That is why I'm cracked you see.
I'm a nut. (clap two times)
I'm a nut. (clap two times)
I'm a nut, I'm a nut, I'm a nut. (tuck yourself into a little ball and roll around on the floor like an acorn)

I'm a little yellow duck,
I like water very much.
Swimming 'round the pond each day,
That is where I'd like to stay.
I'm a duck...quack, quack.
I'm a duck...quack, quack.
I'm a duck, I'm a duck, I'm a duck. (walk, swim, and quack like a duck)

I'm a little shiny frog,
Sitting on a big brown log.
I eat flies and bugs all day,
That is why I croak this way.
I'm a frog...ribbit, ribbit.
I'm a frog...ribbit, ribbit.
I'm a frog, I'm a frog, I'm a frog. (hop and croak like a frog)

4. Talk about animal sounds and characteristics. The verses offer information about acorns, ducks, and frogs. You can use this information to expand children's understanding of animals, habitats, and the natural world.

5. Have animal races with the children. Take turns hopping, waddling, or rolling from one end of the room to the other.

Three Green Speckled Frogs

1. Say the following poem and do the actions.

   Three Green Speckled Frogs
   Three green speckled frogs
   Sat on a speckled log. (squat like a frog)
   Eating some most delicious bugs, (lick your lips)
   YUM YUM! (rub your tummy with your hand)
   One jumped into the pool (jump forward in a frog position)
   Where it was nice and cool (pretend to float in the water)
   Then there were two green speckled frogs. (hold up two fingers)

2. Repeat with two frogs and then one frog. At the end of the verse about one frog, the words are, "Then there were no more speckled frogs."

> **LEARNING POWER!**
>
> **Children will laugh their way to learning about the following skills/concepts:**
>
> Creative movement
> Phonemic awareness
> Sequencing

3. Say the poem again in a "frog" voice.
4. Additional verses:

Three white feathered ducks
Sat on a purple truck
Eating some most delicious bugs—YUM YUM!
One jumped into the pond
Of which he was quite fond.
Then there were two white feathered ducks.

Three pink spotted pigs
Sat on a bunch of twigs
Eating some most delicious slop—YUM YUM!
One rolled into the mud
Where he made quite a thud.
Then there were two pink spotted pigs.

LEARNING POWER!

Children will laugh their way to learning about the following skills/concepts:

Listening
Observation

Let's Go on a Bear Hunt

1. Sit cross-legged on the floor. Each sentence is repeated by one child or a group of children. Do the actions together.

Adult: (slapping hands on knees to make a walking noise) *Let's go on a bear hunt!*
Child: (slapping hands on knees to make a walking noise) *Let's go on a bear hunt!*

Adult: *I'm not afraid!*
Child: *I'm not afraid!*

Adult: *Let's go!*
Child: *Let's go!*

Adult: *Look! I see a wheat field!*
Child: *Look! I see a wheat field!*

Adult: *Can't go under it. Can't go around it.*
Child: (repeat)

Adult: *Have to go through it. All right! Let's go.* (scrape palms together, return to walking noise)

Adult: *Oh look! I see a river!*
Child: (repeat)

Adult: *Can't go over it. Can't go around it.*
Child: (repeat)

Adult: *Have to swim through it. All right! Let's go.* (pretend to swim, return to walking noise)

Adult: *Oh, look! I see a bridge.*
Child: (repeat)

Adult: *Can't go under it. Can't go around it.*
Child: (repeat)

Adult: *Have to walk across it. All right! Let's go.* (pound chest, then return to walking noise)

Adult: *Oh look! I see some mud.*
Child: (repeat)

Adult: *Can't go under it. Can't go around it.*
Child: (repeat)

Adult: *Have to go through it.* (make sucking noise with cupped hands, then return to walking noise)

Adult: *Oh, look! I see a cave!*
Child: (repeat)

Adult: *It's a big cave. We'll have to go inside. All right! Let's go.* (close eyes and put hands out in front)

Adult: *It's dark in here! I feel something furry! Oh, oh! It's a bear! RUN!* (slap knees fast and loud to make running sound)

Adult: *There's the mud! Have to crawl through it!* (make sucking noise with cupped hand, then return to running)

Adult: *There's the bridge! Have to run across it!* (pound chest fast, then return to running)

Adult: *There's the river! Have to swim through it!* (pretend to swim fast, then return to running)

Adult: *There's the wheat field! Have to run through it!* (scrape palms together very fast, then return to running)

Adult: *There's the house! Quick, shut the door!* (Clap hands once to shut the door.)

Adult: *Hooray! We're home safe!*

2. Change the words of "Going on a Bear Hunt" to "Going on a Dinosaur Hunt." The children can determine the ending, or use the following sequence: You can climb a giant fern, jump over a volcano, find a tar pit full of dinosaurs, rescue the dinosaurs in the tar pit, get stuck in the tar pit, or see a T-Rex jump out of the tar pit and chase you home.

Fuzzy Wuzzy

1. Read the following rhyme. Say it together.

Fuzzy Wuzzy
Fuzzy Wuzzy was a bear,
A bear was Fuzzy Wuzzy.
When Fuzzy Wuzzy lost his hair,
He wasn't very fuzzy,
Was he?

2. Explain how bears walk on all fours on the ground.
3. Show the children how to walk on all fours and then together walk like bears.
4. Walk like a bear and say the poem.
5. Say the poem in a "bear" voice.
6. Say the poem as fast as you can.

Chubby Little Snowman

1. Say the following poem and do the actions.

Chubby Little Snowman
A chubby little snowman (hold your arms out, slightly curved)
Had a carrot nose. (point to your nose)
Along came a bunny (hold up two fingers on one hand and fold the others into the palm to make a bunny)
And what do you suppose?
That hungry little bunny (rub your tummy)
Looking for his lunch (shade your eyes with one hand and look around)
Ate that little snowman's nose (pretend to grab nose)
Nibble, nibble, crunch. (pretend to chew on a carrot)

2. Ask the children to move like a chubby snowman. How would a snowman dance? Walk up and down steps? Kick a ball? Can he wiggle his nose, roll in the snow, sit down, and throw a snowball?

The Butcher Shop

1. Say the following poem and do the actions.

   My father owns the butcher shop. (make a big circle with your hands)
   My mother cuts the meat. (pretend to chop)
   And I'm the little hot dog (point to yourself)
   That runs around the street. (run around in a small circle)

2. Additional verses by Jackie Silberg:

   My father owns a shoe store.
   My mother keeps it neat.
   And I'm the little tennis shoe
   That runs around the street.

   My mother owns a great big farm.
   My father harvests wheat.
   And I'm the little piece of bread
   That runs around the street.

3. Make up actions to go with the additional verses. Ask for suggestions.

Flicker, Flicker, Flack

1. Say this poem over and over and move your hands back and forth like windshield wipers. Each time you say the poem, go a little faster. See how fast you can go.

   Flicker, flicker, flack
   Flicker, flicker, flack
   The wipers on the car go
   Flicker, flicker, flack.
   The rain goes flick
   The rain goes flack
   The wipers on the car go
   Flicker, flicker flack.

2. Make up your own rhymes, starting the words with a different consonant. For example,

Clicker, clicker, clack, the train on the track goes clicker, clicker, clack.
(move like a train)
Ticker, ticker, tack, the birds in the trees go ticker, ticker, tack. (fly like a bird)

Five Little Snowmen

1. Say the following poem and do the actions.

   Five little snowmen riding on the sled (pretend five fingers are sledding)
   One fell off and bumped his head. (pretend one finger falls off... rub head)
   I called Frosty and Frosty said, (dial imaginary telephone)
   "No more snowmen riding on that sled!" (say in deep voice)

2. Continue counting down, "Four little snowmen..." and so on.
3. Act out the poem with the children. Sit on the floor and pretend to be in a horse-drawn sleigh.

> **LEARNING POWER!**
>
> **Children will laugh their way to learning about the following skills/concepts:**
>
> Coordination
> Sequencing

The Snow-key Pokey

1. The Hokey Pokey can be used in many ways and can fit many different themes.
2. For a winter unit, do the Snow-key Pokey, and put your snowflake, mitten, boot, or snowball in and out.
3. Some other ideas are:
   Money—your penny, nickel, dime, quarter, and dollar in and out.
   Language—substitute foreign words for the body parts, such as Spanish, French, and Italian (see the chart).

English	Spanish	French	Italian
head	cabeza	la tête	la testa
foot	el pie	le pied	il iede
elbow	el codo	le coude	il gomito
shoulder	el hombro	l'epaule	la spalla
knee	la rodilla	le genou	il ginocchio
hip	la cadera	la hanche	il fianco
whole body	el cuerpo entero	le corps entier	il corpo intero

4. Sometimes you can find appropriate manipulatives to use in the dance: for a farm animal unit, hand out toy animals, and put your cows, horses, and pigs in and out!

The Folded Man

1. When introducing the following poem, curl into a ball, and then as you say the poem, unfold limb by limb until flat on the floor.

The Folded Man
Have you heard of the man
Who stood on his head,
And put his clothes
Into his bed,
And folded himself
On a chair instead?

2. Sit down and say the rhyme.

3. Say it again and together act out the words.

4. Fold yourself up as if you were the man in the rhyme.

5. Stand in unusual ways, such as on one foot, on one foot and one hand, and on all fours.

6. For the ultimate challenge, stand on your head! Help as needed.

Once There Was a Snowman

> **LEARNING POWER!**
>
> **Children will laugh their way to learning about the following skills/concepts:**
>
> Coordination

1. Say the following poem and do the actions.

Once There Was a Snowman

Once there was a snowman (stand straight with your arms out, like a snowman)
Who stood outside my door.
He thought he'd like to come inside (take one step forward)
And run around the floor. (run in a circle in place)
He thought he'd like to warm himself (hold your hands out before an imaginary fire)
By the fireside red.
He thought he'd like to climb upon a big white, cozy bed. (pretend to climb)

So he asked the North Wind,
"Won't you help me play? (clasp your hands and look sad)
I'm completely frozen (hug yourself and shiver)
Standing here all day." (stand rigid, with your arms out)
So the north wind came along (lean to one side, as if you are being
    blown by the wind)
And blew him in the door.
And now there's nothing left of him (slowly sink to the floor)
But a puddle on the floor.

2. Talk about what happened to the snowman.
3. If possible, bring some snow inside and watch it melt when you blow on it.

LEARNING POWER!

Children will laugh their way to learning about the following skills/concepts:

Creativity/Imagination

The Little Sausages

1. Say the following poem.
2. Repeat the poem and act it out together.

The Little Sausages
A hungry boy went walking,
And walked into a store.
He bought a pound of sausages
And laid them on the floor.

The boy began to whistle,
He whistled up a tune,
And all the little sausages
Danced around the room.

3. Put on some music and pretend to be sausages dancing around the room.
4. This poem provides an excellent opportunity to teach about weights and measures by weighing different amounts of cooked sausages. Keep track of how many sausages equal one pound, two pounds, one-half pound, and so on.
5. When you are finished, eat the sausages! Yum!

Make a Bug

LEARNING POWER!

Children will laugh their way to learning about the following skills/concepts:

Body awareness
Coordination
Creativity/Imagination

1. Give the children paper and crayons or markers.
2. Ask them to draw a circle.
3. Say the following rhyme to the children. Let them decide how many feet, lips, and so on to add to their bug (the circle).

   Add— feet so it can walk.
   Add— lips so it can talk.
   Add— eyes so it can see
   What kind of bug could you be?

   Add— antennae for an earful.
   Add— smiles to make it cheerful.
   Speak to me, bug. What did you say? (let the children make up their
       own silly sounds)
   I'm so glad you are here today.
   —Jackie Silberg

4. After you have read the poem, encourage the children to crawl on the floor like bugs.
5. Emphasize that bugs crawl slowly; be sure the children have enough room to move so as not to run into each other.
6. Try this fun game: Tell the children they are going to crawl like bugs. Tell them that bugs only come out at night. Instruct the children to crawl when the light is off. When you turn the light on, tell them to scurry under a table and "hide" until you turn the light off again.

Group Games and Activities

The following games and activities are fun ways for a group of children to share laughter-filled moments. During these games and activities, the children may also experience "group joy." This is a spontaneous wave of laughter that spreads through a group of children who are playing.

Note: Although the games and activities in this chapter were designed for a group of children, most can be modified for use with one or two children.

The Passing Game

1. Sit in a circle on the floor.
2. Choose three unusual objects to pass around the circle, such as a worn-out tennis shoe, a floppy hat, a rubber duck, or a dog biscuit. Give the objects to three children.
3. Play some music and pass the three objects around the circle in one direction.
4. Choose music that starts slowly and gets faster and faster; circus themes work well for this.
5. Tell the group that, as the music gets faster, they must pass the objects faster. No one may pass more than one object at a time.
6. The object is not to get caught with two objects at the same time.

Stacking Cups

1. Stack paper cups to create a pyramid.
2. Tie a string to a beanbag and hang it from the ceiling, so the bag hangs level with the middle of the pyramid, but several inches away.
3. Let the fun begin! Swing the beanbag and knock over the pyramid, and then start all over again! This activity will help introduce the concept of gravity to the children.

Ping-Pong Ball Blow

1. Children gather around the table (try to have small gaps between children) sitting on the floor, on their knees, or on chairs. They need to be positioned so that their chins are at table level.
2. Place a ping-pong ball in front of one child. This child begins by blowing the ball.
3. The object of the game is to keep the ball on the table without using any hands. Just try to do this without laughing!

> **LEARNING POWER!**
>
> **Children will laugh their way to learning about the following skills/concepts:**
>
> Body awareness
> Coordination
> Socialization

I Can Draw a Circle

1. Say the following poem together. This teaches about circles.

I Can Draw a Circle
I can draw a circle
I can draw it in the air (draw circles in the air)
Round and round
I can draw it everywhere.

I can draw a circle
I can draw it on the floor (draw pretend circles on the floor)
Round and round
I can draw more and more.

I can draw a circle
I can draw it on your back (children use their fingers to draw circles on each other's backs)
Round and round
I'll make you giggle
If you wiggle!
—Jackie Silberg

2. Draw circles on legs, arms, neck, and top of the head.

> **LEARNING POWER!**
>
> **Children will laugh their way to learning about the following skills/concepts:**
>
> Body awareness
> Socialization

The Choo-Choo Train

LEARNING POWER!

Children will laugh their way to learning about the following skills/concepts:

Creative movement

1. Designate one child to be the engine of the train. The other children line up, single file, behind the first child.
2. Play some "train" music (see suggestions below) and ask the engine to walk in a silly way, making silly movements with his arms, legs, head, or other body parts.
3. Demonstrate some silly movements. For example, stick your tongue out, walk pigeon-toed, or wiggle your elbows.
4. The group imitates the engine's silly movements.
5. Give each child a chance to be the engine.
6. Some ideas for music to accompany this activity include "She'll be Comin' 'Round the Mountain," "The Orange Blossom Special," and "The Wabash Cannonball." You can find these songs on many different children's music CDs, such as *Song and Play Time With Pete Seeger* by Pete Seeger (Smithsonian Folkways), *American Folk, Game and Activity Songs for Children* by Pete Seeger (Smithsonian Folkways) *Orange Blossom Special* by Johnny Cash (Sony), or *The Very Best of Roy Acuff: Wabash Cannonball* by Roy Acuff (Collectables). Or search online for train songs at one of the children's songs websites, such as www.kididdles.com.

Guess Who?

1. Take photos of the children that do not fully show their faces. For instance, show them peeking out from behind a chair, or show the backs of their heads, close-ups of only part of their faces, or only their feet.

2. Put these pictures together to make a "Guess Who?" book. You can follow each partial photograph with a complete photo of the child, to serve as the answer to the guess.

3. This is an especially good activity to help children learn the names of the others in the group.

4. Seeing photographs of friends in which the photos are taken at different angles, as well as seeing different parts of their bodies, is very humorous to children. It might be fun to let each child take an unusual photograph of another child. Develop the film and the children will truly enjoy seeing their photographic work.

Magic Wand

1. Make a magic wand from rolled-up paper or buy a commercial one.
2. Sit in a circle with the children and say:

   Abracadabra
   Ziggety Zee
   You can be a _____.

3. Point the wand at one child and tell him or her what to be. The child acts out the suggestion. Animals are good beginning ideas.

4. Young children love silly language. Try making up a silly name like "Hobbledy Gobbledy" and see how the child decides to act out that name.

5. Another silly idea might be to name an animal moving in an unusual way, such as a frog hopping backwards or a tiger ice skating.

The Park in the Dark

1. Closing your eyes and imagining things will always lead to humorous ideas and experiences. Take an imaginary trip to the park in the dark.
2. Ask the group to lie down and close their eyes.
3. Make noises of things you might hear in the park, such as birds, bees, wind, car horns, bicycle bells, crickets, and so on. Suggest to the children to imagine *where* the sounds are coming from and *what* is making the sound. For example, the bicycle bells could be coming from a tree or a bird could be riding on the bicycle.
4. Children try to guess what sound you are making.
5. They will soon be bursting with suggestions of more noises for you to make, or you can ask them to make the noises.
6. Extend this activity by reading *The Listening Walk* by Paul Showers.
7. Do this game with other environments such as the zoo, the beach, and so on.

What Am I Doing?

1. Pretend to use an imaginary object.
2. Children guess what you are doing. Suggestions include:

   ★ Peel a banana
   ★ Hammer a nail
   ★ Drink some milk
   ★ Throw a ball
   ★ Put on a ring

3. This kind of game develops communication skills and cognitive thinking.
4. Suggest that children act out blowing a bubble, jumping on a trampoline, walking like a gorilla, or ask two children to pretend to wash a dog (one is the dog).

Ice Cream Game

1. Cut different colors of felt into circles that are the size of scoops of ice cream. Also cut out felt ice cream cones. Buy or make a flannel board.

2. Give each child a felt circle and tell this story.

   One very hot day, Beni (use a child's name) *wanted some ice cream. He went to the ice cream store and said to the lady behind the counter, "May I please have an ice cream cone?"*
   "Yes," said the lady, "What flavor would you like?"
   "I don't know," said Beni.
   The lady said, "Here, try this flavor." (Put your cone on the felt board, and take a flavor from one child. Ask that child to decide what flavor his circle is.)
   Beni took a lick. (Ask the children to make a licking sound as if eating ice cream.) *"Mmmm! That's good!" said Beni, "I like* (flavor) *ice cream, but it's not my favorite flavor."*
   So the lady gave him another flavor to try. (Ask another child to give you a circle and tell you the flavor. Put another circle on top of the first, like a double scoop.) *Beni took a lick of the* (flavor) *ice cream and then the* (flavor) *ice cream and he said, "Mmmm! That's good! But it's not my favorite flavor."*

3. Continue the story, adding each child's circle to the cone, asking him or her to decide the flavor, and reciting all the flavors each time. The children will help you remember what they are!
   When you reach the final flavor, have everyone help take an extra-big lick of the [very long name] ice cream cone and then say:

   When Beni tasted that, he said "Wow! Now THAT is my favorite flavor! I'll take another, please!"

4. Stacking the scoops and trying to say such a long name is funny to children and is also great for their language skills.

Simple Charades

1. Ask one child in the group to think of an animal and then tell you what animal she is thinking of.
2. Ask if anyone would like to show the group how that animal walks. If no one volunteers, demonstrate for the group.
3. Explain how you are going to pretend to be another animal and let them guess the name of the animal. Start with something simple with a recognizable sound such as a cow, dog, cat, or duck.
4. Soon the children will want to pretend to be an animal.
5. Encourage taking turns so that each child will get her chance to act out an animal.
6. Once children can do this, they can begin to act out the animal's movements without using the voice.
7. Try using characters from books such as *The Rainbow Fish* or *The Very Hungry Caterpillar*.

Peas Porridge

1. Sit in a circle.
2. Teach the following rhyme to the group.

Peas porridge hot, peas porridge cold,
Peas porridge in the pot, nine days old.
Some like it hot, some like it cold.
Some like it in the pot, nine days old.

3. Ask one child to be the leader.
4. The leader walks around the outside of the circle and taps each child gently on the head while he says the rhyme.
5. The child that the leader taps at the end of the rhyme jumps up and chases the leader around the circle back to the vacant place.
6. The child left without a space becomes the leader.
7. You can play this game with any rhyme or song.

Pass the Potato

1. Sit in a circle.
2. Say the following poem to the rhythm of the song "London Bridges." This activity teaches language skills such as repetition of sounds, awareness of meter and form, and listening for words.

   'Round the circle, here it comes
   Here it comes, here it comes.
   'Round the circle, here it comes
   Pass the potato.

3. As the children say the rhyme, they pass a potato around the circle.
4. When the rhyme is finished, the child left holding the potato comes into the middle of the circle and pretends he is eating it.
5. He can also tell what kind of potato he is eating (mashed, fried, boiled, and so on).
6. Play this game with other kinds of food.

Nursery Rhyme Guessing Game

1. Gather some props that can serve as symbols for various nursery rhymes, such as:

   ★ a mouse for "Hickory, Dickory Dock"
   ★ a spoon for "Hey, Diddle, Diddle"
   ★ a baby doll for "Rock-a-bye, Baby"
   ★ a muffin tin for "Do You Know the Muffin Man?"
   ★ a piggy for "This Little Piggy Went to Market"

2. Hide these props in a bag or box so the children can't see them.
3. Tell the group that they are going to play a guessing game.
4. Pull out one of the objects and ask them to guess which nursery rhyme it comes from.
5. When they have guessed the rhyme, say it together.
6. This is a very satisfying game! Of course, you can read a Mother Goose book beforehand if you think they need a review, or afterwards as a wrap-up.

LEARNING POWER!

Children will laugh their way to learning about the following skills/concepts:

Coordination
Socialization

Blindfolded Beanbag Toss

1. Place an empty box, bucket, or basket an appropriate distance from the group.
2. Let the children toss a beanbag into the container several times, so they know what to do.
3. Use a scarf or handkerchief to blindfold one child at a time.
4. Let her throw beanbags into the container while blindfolded.

LEARNING POWER!

Children will laugh their way to learning about the following skills/concepts:

Coordination

Bowling Alley

1. Make sure there is plenty of room for this activity.
2. Use 10 two-liter empty plastic bottles as the bowling pins.
3. Make a template, if desired, in a traditional pattern. It's nice but not necessary to have a cardboard template to set up the pins.
4. Ask the group what they think will happen if you roll a large rubber ball into the pins.
5. Roll the ball and see how many pins get knocked down
6. Count the pins each time (do not, however, keep score).
7. Try other patterns for setting up the pins, inventing your own designs, or try different sizes or types of balls.

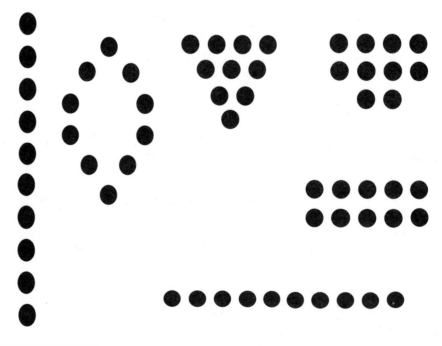

Squirrel in a Tree

1. You will need matching picture cards. Each pair should be different.
2. Divide the children into two groups and designate one group as "trees" and the other as "squirrels."
3. Give each "tree" a picture card and each "squirrel" the matching picture cards.
4. Ask the "trees" to move to various parts of the room and remain stationary.
5. Say, "Squirrel in a tree!" and the "squirrels" must move around and find their matching "tree." This will help children learn about opposites. The squirrels will know which tree is their match by looking at the trees.

Ball in the Box Game

1. Cut a hole in the center of a large box, such as a large gift box or a copy paper box.
2. Two children stand up, each holding one end of the box.
3. Another child drops a ball (golf ball or ping-pong ball) into the box near one end.
4. The children who are holding the box move it back and forth and try to roll the ball into the hole.
5. This game takes a lot of cooperation and it is a great deal of fun.

1.

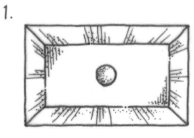

Top View

2.

Where's Your Elbow?

1. This game reinforces the names of body parts.
2. Play this game with one other person or divide the children into pairs.
3. Name a body part and ask your partner to show you the same body part on his body. For example, elbow. You show your elbow and your partner shows his elbow.
4. Now, touch your elbow to your partner's elbow.
5. Repeat with a different body part such as your toes.

Duck, Duck, Goose

1. This popular game never loses its magic.
2. Sit in a circle and choose one child to be "it."
3. "It" walks around the circle and taps each child on the head, saying the word "duck."
4. When she taps someone on the head and says the word "goose," that child gets up and runs around the circle trying to catch "it."
5. If the child who is "it" sits down in the empty spot before she is tagged, the new child becomes "it."
6. Ask the children to come up with silly names, such as, "baseball, baseball, football" or "worm, worm, slug."

I've a Wagon

1. Teach this poem to a group of children.
2. Encourage them to make the sounds of the animals as the animals are mentioned in the poem.
3. Divide the children into small groups.
4. Assign each group one animal sound. If you let the groups make the animal sounds all at the same time, they will enjoy this very much.

I've a wagon full of chickens that are cackling and squawking.
With my wagon full of chickens, I would rather be walking.
It's cackle, cackle, cackle, squawk, squawk,
It's cackle, cackle, cackle squawk, squawk.

I've a wagon full of ducklings who are flapping and quacking.
I've a wagon full of ducklings who are flapping and quacking.
It's flap, flap, flap, quack, quack, quack,
It's flap, flap, flap, quack, quack, quack.

5. Additional verses:

I've a wagon full of horses
Who are whinnying and neighing.
With my wagon full of horses,
I can't hear what I'm saying!
It's whinny, whinny, whinny, neigh, neigh…

I've a wagon full of donkeys
Who are braying and kicking.
With my wagon full of donkeys,
How my ears take a licking!
It's hee-haw, hee-haw, hee-haw, kick, kick . . .

Father's Whiskers

1. Explain that a conductor tells the rest of the musicians when and how to play their instruments.
2. Everyone watches closely while you demonstrate the following movements: Stretch your arms out in front of you and direct the change from loud to soft and soft to loud in the following manner:
   Loud: Raise your arms, palms up.
   Soft: Lower your arms, palms down.
3. Teach the chorus and let the children practice singing it several times.
4. Sing the song and everyone joins in on the chorus.
5. Sing the song again and signal for the children to sing the chorus softly.
6. Sing again, this time singing the chorus loudly.

Father's Whiskers
(Tune: "99 Bottles of Pop")
I have a dear old daddy,
For whom I nightly pray,
He has a set of whiskers
That are always in the way.

LEARNING POWER!

Children will laugh their way to learning about the following skills/concepts:

Creativity/Imagination

Chorus:
Oh, they're always in the way,
The cows eat them for hay,
They hide the dirt on Daddy's shirt,
They're always in the way.

Father had a strong back,
Now it's all caved in,
He stepped upon his whiskers
And walked up to his chin.

Chorus

Father has a daughter,
Her name is Ella Mae,
She climbs up father's whiskers
And braids them all the way.

Chorus

I have a dear old mother,
She likes the whiskers, too,
She uses them for dusting
And cleaning out the flue.

Chorus

LEARNING POWER!

Children will laugh their way to learning about the following skills/concepts:

Emotions
Empathy
Observation

It's Funny, My Puppy

1. This game requires at least two children or a group of children divided into pairs.
2. Ask one partner in each pair to be the "puppy" and the other one to be the "master."
3. Tell the partners to act out the rhyme as follows:
   When the master smiles, the puppy yaps and rolls on the floor.
   When the master frowns, the puppy slumps down.

It's funny,
My puppy
Knows just how I feel.

When I'm happy
He's yappy
And squirms like an eel.

When I'm grumpy
He's slumpy
And stays at my heel.

It's funny
My puppy
Knows such a great deal.

4. Switch parts.
5. Talk about how animals express their feelings. Have they ever seen a dog that was frightened or angry? How did the dog behave?

Simon Senses

1. Play the game "Simon Says" using the five senses. For example:

   ★ When Simon says "hear," you must touch your ears. (Simon says, "Hear the wind.")
   ★ When Simon says "see," you must point to your eyes. (Simon says, "See the flowers.")
   ★ When Simon says "taste," you must stick out your tongue. (Simon says, "Taste the nutmeg.")
   ★ When Simon says "smell," you must touch your nose. (Simon says, "Smell the apple.")
   ★ When Simon says "touch," you must wiggle your fingers. (Simon says, "Touch your nose.")

A Fishy Feltboard

LEARNING POWER!

Children will laugh their way to learning about the following skills/concepts:

Cognitive thinking

1. Using felt, cut out enough little fish so that each child can hold one. Call the children in the group "little fishes."
2. Cut one for you, or find yourself a fish toy or puppet.
3. Your fish is the Teacher Fish, who will be admitting little fishies into her "school of fish."
4. Ask questions that the children can answer, such as, "How much is one plus one?" and "What animal says 'neigh'?" and "Who lives in a cave?"
5. The Teacher Fish poses a question and calls upon one Little Fish to answer it. If the child gets it right, he or she adds his or her fish to the felt board, joining the "school." The teacher can ask silly questions too, such as:

   ★ How does a dog meow?
   ★ Can a banana swim?
   ★ Can a truck talk?

6. Continue until all the "fish" are in school.
7. End the game by singing a fish song such as "Three Little Fishies" or make up your own fish song.

On My Birthday

1. The first child says, "On my birthday I want a doll."
2. The next child says, "On my birthday I want a doll and a tricycle."
3. The next child says the same as the second child and then adds a third item.
4. This game is very challenging and also very funny. Sometimes the children laugh at the items that are mentioned as birthday presents. They can also say funny things such as, "On my birthday I want a gorilla." This activity develops sequencing and memory skills in a fun way. Sequencing experiences are essential building blocks for reading.

> **LEARNING POWER!**
>
> **Children will laugh their way to learning about the following skills/concepts:**
>
> Sequencing

Guess the Sound

1. Demonstrate all the different sounds that you can make with your body. Pound your fists on your chest, stamp your feet, snap your fingers, and so on.
2. Ask the children in the group to hide their eyes and guess what body sound you are making.
3. Or, choose a child to make a body sound while the others listen with their eyes closed.
4. Whoever identifies the sound first gets to be the next leader.

> **LEARNING POWER!**
>
> **Children will laugh their way to learning about the following skills/concepts:**
>
> Listening

Boiling Hot

1. This is a popular word game that encourages creativity.
2. Talk about the different things that might go into a witch's pot to make a witch's brew.
3. Include gruesome ingredients such as "spider legs."
4. Say this rhyme:

   Boiling hot, boiling hot
   What will you put in the witch's pot?

5. Choose one child at a time to share his idea. Show him how to incorporate his idea into the rhyme.

   Boiling hot, boiling hot
   I'll put spider legs in the witch's pot.

6. When it's time to end the game, say:

   Boiling hot, boiling hot
   We are through with the witch's pot.

Let's Make a Salad

1. If possible, get a chef's hat to play this game.
2. Sit in a circle.
3. Choose one child to be the chef. The chef stands in the middle of the circle.
4. Each child sitting in the circle decides what food he or she would like to be for the salad.
5. Go around the circle and let each child tell you the name of a food. Help those who need it.
6. Say to the chef, "Chef, would you like some lettuce in your salad?" The chef answers, "Yes, I would like some lettuce in my salad."
7. Whoever is the lettuce (it can be more than one person) gets up and goes into the middle of the circle and stands next to the chef.
8. Continue until every child is in the middle of the circle.
9. Then say, "Toss the salad!" Everyone jumps up and down until you say, "Time to eat the salad."
10. Everyone sits down and pretends to eat the salad.

The Birthday Game

LEARNING POWER!

Children will laugh their way to learning about the following skills/concepts:

Listening

1. Young children love to talk about their birthdays.
2. Sit in a circle and select one child at a time.
3. The group says the following poem:

   Apples, peaches, pears and plums
   Tell me when your birthday comes.
   January, February, March, April, May, June, July, August, September,
   October, November, December.

4. When that particular child's birthday month is mentioned, she stands up and does a trick. The trick can be some kind of movement such as jumping, hopping, turning, or anything else the child wants to do.
5. Start the poem again with another child.

What Animal Is That?

LEARNING POWER!

Children will laugh their way to learning about the following skills/concepts:

Listening

1. This is a marvelous listening game that helps children learn to discriminate between sounds.
2. Choose two children from the group. Ask them to turn around so the rest of the group cannot see their faces.
3. Ask each child to think of an animal sound, but not tell anyone what his or her sound is. At the signal (ring a bell, flick the lights, snap your fingers) the two children begin to make their animal sounds over and over until you signal them to stop. (They will make their sounds simultaneously.) The rest of the children listen and tell what sounds they hear.
4. When the group identifies the sounds, those children sit down and two more children get to make an animal sound.
5. After this game has been played several times with two children, you can increase it to three, and eventually four children.
6. Because letting them choose their own sounds is important to their creativity, allow the children to continue if two of them make the same sound.

A Different Simon

1. This is a different version of Simon Says.
2. Instead of Simon doing actions, Simon makes sounds. Simon says, "Cough." Simon says, "Sneeze." Simon says, "Laugh," and so on.
3. Instead of saying Simon, let the leader use his own name, make up silly names, or use funny names of characters from children's books.

Beanbag Hello

1. Have the children sit in a circle, and put on some recorded music.
2. The children pass a beanbag around the circle until you stop the music. When the music stops, the child holding the beanbag says her name in a silly voice.
3. The group responds by saying "Hi!" imitating the child's silly voice.
4. Start the music and pass the beanbag again.
5. Before you play the game, talk about all the different kinds of voices you can use: high, low, fast, slow, crying, laughing, or baby talk.

Something's Drastic

1. Divide the group into two parts.
2. The first group repeats, "Something's drastic" continuously. You might want to have a discussion about the word "drastic."
3. While one group is chanting, "Something's drastic," the second group says the following words and acts them out.

   My ears are elastic.
   My nose is made of plastic.
   I'M FANTASTIC!

4. This is fun to say, to do, and to hear!
5. Repeat each time saying it faster and faster. Then stop suddenly!

Chapter 7

Animal Games and Activities

LEARNING POWER!

Children will laugh their way to learning about the following skills/concepts:

Body awareness
Cognitive thinking
Coordination
Creative movement
Creativity/Imagination
Dramatic play
Emotions
Empathy
Eye-hand coordination
Letter recognition
Listening
Observation
Phonemic awareness
Rhyming
Rhythm
Sequencing
Socialization
Vocabulary

Most children love animals and can empathize with the feelings of animals. This chapter explores the world of animals in funny ways that children can understand and enjoy.

Animals make wonderful subjects for playful learning. For example, when saying the poem "This Little Cow" (page 112), children could say "moo" every time you say the word "cow." Try the same idea with any game or activity that mentions one or more animals.

This Little Cow

1. Say the rhyme and do the actions with your fingers.

This Little Cow
This little cow eats grass. (hold up one hand, fingers erect, and bend down one finger)
This little cow eats hay. (bend down another finger)
This little cow drinks water. (bend down another finger)
And this little cow runs away. (bend down another finger)
This little cow does nothing (bend down last finger)
But lie and sleep all day. (make snoring noise)

2. Say the rhyme and move the fingers of a doll or stuffed animal.
3. For a healthy chuckle, try this game with your toes.

Froggies

1. Hold up one hand with fingers upright and point to one finger at a time with your other hand as you say the poem.

This little froggie hurt his toe.
This little froggie said,"Oh, oh, oh." (say the words in a sad voice)
This little froggie laughed and was glad. (laugh out loud)
This little froggie cried and was sad. (pretend to cry)
This little froggie did just what he should,
Hopped straight to his mother as fast as he could. (hop your fingers away)

2. Talk about things that make you laugh or cry.
3. Make up sentences and either laugh or cry about what you say. For example, "We are going to the zoo," or "I have a tummy ache."

Algie Met a Bear

1. Say the following poem.

Algie met a bear.
The bear met Algie.
The bear was bulgy.
The bulge was Algie.

2. Ask what happened to Algie.
3. If possible, take the children to the zoo to see some live bears. Most zoos house a variety of bears, such as black bears, polar bears, and even grizzly bears. Imitate the bear behaviors you see at the zoo. Growl and walk like bears!
4. Have a bear party with teddy bears or other stuffed animals. Serve honey and graham crackers. Sing bear songs at the party, such as "The Bear Went Over the Mountain" and "The Other Day I Saw a Bear (The Bear Song)."

LEARNING POWER!

Children will laugh their way to learning about the following skills/concepts:

Creativity/Imagination

INTERESTING FACTS ABOUT BEARS INCLUDE:

★ **Bears are found in the Arctic, Asia, Europe, and North and South America.**

★ **Male bears are called boars; female bears are called sows; young bears are called cubs. A group of bears is called a pack or sloth.**

★ **Despite popular belief, bears do not hibernate. Instead, they sleep for short periods during the winter. Bears often wake up and walk around on mild winter days.**

★ **Bears are primarily meat-eating animals, or carnivores. They hunt for mice and ground squirrels in the forests, and they catch fish in the streams. But their diet also includes berries, acorns, nuts, and, of course—honey!**

Ducky Daddles

1. The following poem is so much fun to say.

   Ducky Daddles
   Loves the puddles
   How he waddles
   As he paddles
   In the puddles—
   Ducky Daddles

2. Walk like a duck as
   you say the poem.
   This will generate a
   lot of laughter from
   the children.

3. Pretend to swim in the water, and then shake the water off of your feathers when you waddle out of the water.

4. Sing songs about ducks, such as " Ducky Duddle" and "The Little White Duck," or read a duck story, such as *The Ugly Duckling* by Hans Christian Andersen.

Cats Sleep Anywhere

1. Say the following poem about cats.

   Cats Sleep Anywhere
   Cats sleep anywhere,
   Any table, any chair,
   Top of piano, window-ledge,
   In the middle, on the edge,
   Open drawer, empty shoe,
   Anybody's lap will do.
   Fitted in a cardboard box,
   In the cupboard with your frocks —
   Anywhere! They don't care!
   Cats sleep anywhere.

2. Pretend to be a cat and "meow" around the room.

3. Ask a child to be the cat and give directions where to sleep, such as "Kitty cat, can you sleep under the table?"

Arabella Miller

1. Crawl your fingers up the child's arm as you sing the first verse of the following song.
2. When you sing, "Arabella Miller, take away your caterpillar," shake your index finger back and forth.
3. Sing the second verse standing up. Pretend to crawl up a tree with your arms and when you say, "And fell down on you and me," fall to the ground.
4. Again, on the words "Arabella Miller, take away your caterpillar," shake your index finger back and forth.
5. You can also crawl on the floor as you sing the song.

Little Arabella Miller
(Tune: "Twinkle, Twinkle Little Star")
Little Arabella Miller
Found a fuzzy caterpillar.
First it crawled upon her mother.
Then it crawled upon her brother.
Little Arabella Miller,
Take away your caterpillar.

Arabella did not take it.
She decided to forsake it.
So it crawled up on the tree
And fell down on you and me.
Please, dear Arabella Miller,
Take away your caterpillar.

> **LEARNING POWER!**
>
> **Children will laugh their way to learning about the following skills/concepts:**
>
> Creative movement
> Dramatic play
> Rhyming
> Vocabulary

The Bear Went Over the Mountain

1. Sing this popular song and do the actions.

The Bear Went Over the Mountain
The bear went over the mountain, (make a fierce face and "claws" with your fingers; then make a mountain shape in front of you, arms arched, fingertips touching)
The bear went over the mountain, (repeat)

> **LEARNING POWER!**
>
> **Children will laugh their way to learning about the following skills/concepts:**
>
> Creativity/Imagination

The bear went over the mountain, (repeat)
To see what he could see. (shade your eyes with your hand and look from side to side)

2. Ask, "What do you think he saw?"
3. Sing:

The other side of the mountain, (point behind you; then make a mountain shape in front of you, arms arched, fingertips touching)
The other side of the mountain, (repeat)
The other side of the mountain, (repeat)
Was all that he could see. (shade your eyes with your hand and peer from side to side)

4. Encourage the children to imagine what kinds of things the bear might see on the other side of the mountain. For example, perhaps he might see a great big ocean, or a city, or maybe just a lot of trees. Remember to keep the element of laughter involved in this activity. For example, the bear saw the three bears and Goldilocks climbing a tree, a baby bear driving a fire engine, or a banana and a pear playing the guitar.
5. Sing the song using these new ideas in the second verse. After you say the words, "What do you think he saw," sing, "he saw a beautiful city," or "he saw a shopping mall," and so on.

LEARNING POWER!

Children will laugh their way to learning about the following skills/concepts:

Rhyming

I Know a House

1. Say the rhyme and then repeat each line and act it out.
2. "Shiver" each time you say the word "cold." Children will learn about the concept of cold when you say this rhyme with them.

I know a house, and a cold, old house,
And a cold, old house by the sea.
If I were a mouse in that cold, old house,
What a cold, old mouse I'd be.

3. Change the words. Instead of saying "cold, old," say "nice, warm" to teach the concepts of hot and cold.
4. Talk about how a mouse might use a cane to walk or what a mouse might wear to keep warm.

I See a Little Mouse

1. Say the following fingerplay and do the actions.

    I see a little mouse, (scan the room with one hand shading an eye)
    But he doesn't see me. (shake your head)
    If he could see me (scan the room, as above)
    How frightened he would be. (jump back and look frightened)

    Off he would flee (run in place)
    To his little wee house,
    Then there'd only be me (point to yourself)
    And there wouldn't be mouse. (shake your head)

Pussycat Ate the Dumplings

1. Say the following poem.

    Pussycat ate the dumplings,
    Pussycat ate the dumplings!
    Mama stood by, and cried, "Oh, fie!
    Why did you eat the dumplings?"

2. Explain what a dumpling is. (A dumpling is a small mound of sweet dough with a fruit mixture inside that is baked.)
3. Ask, "Why do you think the pussycat ate the dumplings?"
4. Offer silly suggestions to encourage creative thinking. For example:

    ★ He thought they were round, fat, tasty mice morsels.
    ★ He wanted to feel them roll around in his belly.

Rhymes About Pigs

1. Say the following silly pig rhymes and then repeat them together.

Riddle cum diddle cum dinky,
My little pig's name is Winky;
I keep him quite clean
With the washing machine,
And I rinse him all off in the sinkie.

Hickory, dickory, dare,
A pig flew up in the air.
A man called Brown
Soon fetched him down.
Hickory, dickory, dare.

Higglety, pigglety, pop!
The dog has eaten the mop.
The pig's in a hurry,
The cat's in a flurry,
Higglety, pigglety, pop!

Two Riddle Cum Diddles

1. Say the following rhymes and then repeat them together.

Riddle cum diddle cum dido
My little dog's name is Fido,
I bought him a wagon
And hitched up a dragon
And off we both went for a drive-oh!

Riddle cum diddle cum doodle
My little cat's name is Toodle
I curled up her hair
But she only said, "There!
You have made me look just like a poodle!"

Maggie

1. Say the poem and then repeat it together and do the following actions:

   There was a young maiden called Maggie, (stand in place and curtsy)
   Whose dog was enormous and shaggy. (shake all over)
   The front end of him looked ferocious and grim, (make a ferocious face and growl)
   But the tail end was friendly and waggy. (wag your "tail"!)

Spiders

1. Say the following rhyme. This will help children learn about spiders.

   The eensy weensy spider crawled up the waterspout.
   Down came the rain and washed the spider out.
   Out came the sun and dried up all the rain,
   And the eensy weensy spider climbed up the spout again.

   The eensy weensy spider was climbing up the trees.
   Down came the snow and made the spider freeze.
   Out came the sun and melted all the snow,
   So the eensy weensy spider had another go!

2. If possible, collect several small, crawling insects, such as spiders or beetles, in glass jars.
3. Observe the insects' movements.
4. Imitate the way the insects crawl.
5. Ask, "What kind of shoes would a spider wear? How many pairs of shoes would she need? How would a spider walk in high heels?"

Music Games and Activities

Music and laughter can break down barriers and make it easy to communicate with others. The following games and activities have humorous words or are sung in a funny manner, producing laughter and enjoyment for all.

A fun thing to do with any song is to take one line of a familiar song and sing each syllable backwards. When the children hear the melody, they will recognize the song and enjoy hearing the words backwards. For example, "Twinkle, Twinkle Little Star" is "elk n iwt, elk n iwt, elt til rats" backwards.

Music is the key to learning. It can be used to teach many subjects, including math and languages. It helps develop cognitive learning skills that children need for all types of learning, in addition to being just plain fun and exciting!

Be Kind to Your Web-Footed Friends

1. Sing the following song.

   Be Kind to Your Web-Footed Friends
   (Tune: "Stars and Stripes Forever")
   Be kind to your web-footed friends,
   For that duck may be somebody's mother.
   Be kind to your friends in the swamp
   Where the weather is cold and damp. (rhyme with swamp)
   You may think that this is the end;
   Well it is!

2. March like ducks and quack to the melody instead of singing the words.
3. Imagine that you are birds that live in or near water. What would the birds eat? What kind of sounds would they make?
4. Tell some "ducky" riddles:

   What does a duck eat for snack?
   Cheese and quackers!

The Ants Go Marching

1. March around the room and sing the song. Act out each part that says, "The little one stops to..."

The Ants Go Marching
The ants go marching one by one, hurrah, hurrah
The ants go marching one by one, hurrah, hurrah
The ants go marching one by one
The little one stops to suck his thumb
And they all go marching down
Into the ground
To get out of the rain
Boom, boom, boom.

Additional verses:
two by two… the little one stops to tie his shoe
three by three… the little one stops to climb a tree
four by four… the little one stops to fall on the floor
five by five… the little one stops to joke and jive
six by six… the little one stops to do some tricks
seven by seven… the little one stops to point to heaven
eight by eight… the little one stops to shut the gate
nine by nine… the little one stops to read a sign
ten by ten… the little one stops to say "THE END."

2. Substitute other actions for the word marching, as follows:

The ants go skipping…
The ants go hopping…
The ants go swimming…

3. Experiment with ant voices. Tiny, squeaky voices are lots of fun.
4. Party stores carry plastic ants. Singing and counting the ants as you move them along is a great game.

LEARNING POWER!

Children will laugh their way to learning about the following skills/concepts:

Coordination

Little Peter Rabbit

1. Sing the following words and do the actions.

Little Peter Rabbit
(Tune: "Battle Hymn of the Republic")
Little Peter Rabbit had a fly upon his ear. (point to your ear)
Little Peter Rabbit had a fly upon his ear.
Little Peter Rabbit had a fly upon his ear.
And he flicked it and it flew away. (flick your fingers on your ear)

2. Repeat the song and do the actions. Each time you repeat the song, leave out a word but continue to do all the actions.
   First time—leave out "ear"
   Second time—leave out "ear" and "fly" and pretend to buzz like a fly
   Third time—leave out "ear," "fly," and "Peter Rabbit" and put your hands on your head for rabbit ears
   Fourth time—leave out "ear," "fly," "Peter Rabbit," and "flicked" and flick your fingers
   Fifth time—leave out "ear," "fly," "Peter Rabbit," "flicked," and "flew away" and fly around the room

3. Another version of this song is:

Little Peter Rabbit had a cold upon his chest.
Little Peter Rabbit had a cold upon his chest.
Little Peter Rabbit had a cold upon his chest.
And he rubbed it with camphorated oil.

4. Repeat the song and do the actions as with the first version. Leave out words and do following actions:
First time—leave out "cold" (sneeze)
Second time—leave out "chest" (touch your chest)
Third time—leave out "rubbed" (rub your chest)
Fourth time—leave out "Camphorated oil" (hold your nose as if the oil has a bad smell)

Oh, the Horsie Went Around

LEARNING POWER!

Children will laugh their way to learning about the following skills/concepts:

Coordination

1. Sing the song as you try to move on one foot. Help those who need it.

Oh, the Horsie Went Around
(Tune: "Turkey in the Straw") adapted words by Jackie Silberg
Oh, the horsie went around with his foot off of the ground.
Oh, the horsie went around with his foot off of the ground.
Oh, the horsie went around with his foot off of the ground,
Silly, silly, silly, horsie neigh, neigh, neigh.

2. Sing it again and change the actions.

…with his hand on the ground (bend over and walk with your hand touching the ground)
…knees on the ground (walk on your knees)
…toes off of the ground (walk on your heels)
…heels off of the ground (walk on your toes)

3. Change the words to movement actions such as running, skipping, or hopping.
4. If you really want to be silly, try "tummy on the ground."
5. Remember to say "neigh" in a big voice.

Skin and Bones
(Folk Song from Kentucky)

1. Sing the following song using a spooky voice for the "oo-oo" part. This will help children learn about sounds and sound words.

Skin and Bones

There was an old woman all skin and bones, oo-oo-oo-ooh!
One night she thought she'd take a walk, oo-oo-oo-ooh!
She walked down by the old graveyard, oo-oo-oo-ooh!
She saw the bones a-layin' around, oo-oo-oo-ooh!
She went to the closet to get a broom, oo-oo-oo-ooh!
She opened the door and, BOO!

2. This is a great song to use with rhythm instruments. Experiment with instruments and decide which ones make spooky sounds.
3. This song also is great to act out.

No, No, Yes, Yes
(Tune: "Reveille")

1. Sing the words "no, no" and "yes, yes" to the tune of "Reveille." Talk about how "no" and "yes" are opposites.
2. Sing "no" for the first part of the song and "yes" for the second part of the song.
3. Switch parts.
4. Choose other words that are opposites and sing them to this tune, such as black/white, fast/slow, high/low, hot/cold, and so on.

"Reveille" is a song that the army has used for a wake-up call. Irving Berlin used it in his song "Oh, How I Hate to Get Up in the Morning." In this song, the words "You gotta get up, you gotta get up, you gotta get up in the morning" are sung to the tune of "Reveille."

The Alphabet Song

1. Learning the alphabet is a key pre-reading skill.
2. When you sing the alphabet song, your voice draws attention to the letters of the alphabet.
3. Make eye contact and begin singing the alphabet song: *"A-B-C-D (pause) E-F-G (pause) H-I-J-K (pause) L-M-N-O-P (pause) Q-R-S (pause) T-U-V (pause) W-X (pause) Y and Z. Now I've sung my ABC's, next time won't you sing with me?"*
4. For a change, sing this song very slowly or very fast.
5. Now sing the song in a high, peeping voice (like a bird) or with a deep, dark voice (like a bear.)

> **LEARNING POWER!**
>
> **Children will laugh their way to learning about the following skills/concepts:**
>
> Letter recognition

I Love a Parade

1. Turn hands into flags by rubber stamping them with a flag stamp or applying flag stickers.
2. Wave your hands from side to side so they look like flags flapping in the breeze.
3. Play some marching music and wave your "flags" to the music.
4. Read a parade book such as Gene Baer's *Thump Thump Rat-a-Tat-Tat* or *Parade* by Donald Crews. Wave your hand "flags" for the parade in the story.

> **LEARNING POWER!**
>
> **Children will laugh their way to learning about the following skills/concepts:**
>
> Listening

Mardi Gras Party

1. Make some simple masks using paper plates or craft paper and decorate with glitter and feathers.
2. Put on some Dixieland music and march around the room to have your own Mardi Gras parade!

Michael Finnegan

1. Enjoy singing this silly song with the children.

Michael Finnegan
(Tune: "My Little Red Wagon")
There was an old man called Michael Finnegan.
He grew whiskers on his chinnegan.
Pulled them out but they grew inegan,
Poor old Michael Finnegan.
Beginnegan.

There was an old man called Michael Finnegan.
He went fishing with a pinnegan.
He caught a fish but dropped it inegan,
Poor old Michael Finnegan.
Beginnegan.

There was an old man called Michael Finnegan
He grew fat and then grew thinegan,
Then he died and had to beginegan,
Poor old Michael Finnegan.

Bibliography

Brewton, J. 1989. *My tang's tungled: And other ridiculous situations*, reprint edition. New York: HarperCollins Juvenile Books.

Cole, J. 1989. *Anna banana: 101 jump rope rhymes.* New York: William Morrow.

Conte, Y.F. *Serious laughter: Live a happier, healthier, more productive life.* 1998. Rochester, NY: Amsterdam-Berwick Publishing.

Cousins, N. *Anatomy of an illness as perceived by the patient: Reflections on healing and regeneration.* New York: Bantam Doubleday Dell.

Deshpande, C. & J. Eccleshare. 1994. *Spring tinderbox: Festivals, poems, stories, songs and activities*, spiral edition. 1994. London, UK: A&C Black.

Emrich, D. 1975. *Whim wham book.* New York: Simon & Schuster.

Freud, S. & J. Strachey. 1963. *Jokes and their relation to the unconscious.* New York: W.W. Norton & Company.

Holden, R. 1999. *Laughter the best medicine: The healing powers of happiness, humour, and joy!* London, UK: Thorsons Publishing.

Hunt, B., ed. 1998. *Count me in: 44 songs and rhymes about numbers.* London, UK: A&C Black.

Klein, A. 1989. *The healing power of humor: Techniques for getting through loss, setbacks, upsets, disappointments, difficulties, trials, tribulations, and all that.* New York: J. P. Tarcher.

Klein, A. 1998. *The courage to laugh: Humor, hope, and healing in the face of death and dying.* New York: J. P. Tarcher.

Low, J. 1983. *Beastly riddles.* New York: Atheneum.

McGhee, P. 1980. *Humor, its origin and development.* New York: W.H. Freeman & Co.

Nelson, E. 1981. *The silly songbook.* New York: Sterling Publications.

O'Donnell, R. 1997. *Kids are punny: Jokes sent by kids to the Rosie O'Donnell Show.* New York: Warner Books.

McKee, D. 1994., ill. *Okki-tokki-unga.* London, England : A & C Black (Publishers) Ltd.

Opie, P. & I. Opie, Eds. 1991. *Tail feathers from Mother Goose: The Opie rhyme book.* New York: Little, Brown & Co.

Phipps, B. 1991. *Singing with young children* (Book and Cassette edition). Los Angeles, CA: Alfred Publishing Company.

Rosen, M. 1992. *Sonsense Nongs: Michael Rosen's book of silly songs, daft ditties, crazy croons, loony lyrics, batty ballads, and nutty numbers.* London, UK: A&C Black.

Index

Game Index

Song Index